BACKGROUND SUBSTRACTION MOTION DETECTION TECHNIQUES WITH OPENCV AND TKINTER

VIVIAN SIAHAAN
RISMON HASIHOLAN SIANIPAR

Copyright © 2024 BALIGE Publishing

All rights reserved. No part of this book may be reproduced, stored in a retrieval system, or transmitted in any form or by any means, without the prior written permission of the publisher, except in the case of brief quotations embedded in critical articles or reviews. Every effort has been made in the preparation of this book to ensure the accuracy of the information presented. However, the information contained in this book is sold without warranty, either express or implied. Neither the authors, nor BALIGE Publishing or its dealers and distributors, will be held liable for any damages caused or alleged to have been caused directly or indirectly by this book. BALIGE Publishing has endeavored to provide trademark information about all of the companies and products mentioned in this book by the appropriate use of capitals. However, BALIGE Publishing cannot guarantee the accuracy of this information.

Published: MAY 2024
Production reference: 0100524
Published by BALIGE Publishing Ltd.
BALIGE, North Sumatera

ABOUT THE AUTHOR

Vivian Siahaan is a highly motivated individual with a passion for continuous learning and exploring new areas. Born and raised in Hinalang Bagasan, Balige, situated on the picturesque banks of Lake Toba, she completed her high school education at SMAN 1 Balige. Vivian's journey into the world of programming began with a deep dive into various languages such as Java, Android, JavaScript, CSS, C++, Python, R, Visual Basic, Visual C#, MATLAB, Mathematica, PHP, JSP, MySQL, SQL Server, Oracle, Access, and more. Starting from scratch, Vivian diligently studied programming, focusing on mastering the fundamental syntax and logic. She honed her skills by creating practical GUI applications, gradually building her expertise. One particular area of interest for Vivian is animation and game development, where she aspires to make significant contributions. Alongside her programming and mathematical pursuits, she also finds joy in indulging in novels, nurturing her love for literature. Vivian Siahaan's passion for programming and her extensive knowledge are reflected in the numerous ebooks she has authored. Her works, published by Sparta Publisher, cover a wide range of topics, including "Data Structure with Java," "Java Programming: Cookbook," "C++ Programming: Cookbook," "C Programming For High Schools/Vocational Schools and Students," "Java Programming for SMA/SMK," "Java Tutorial: GUI, Graphics and Animation," "Visual Basic Programming: From A to Z," "Java Programming for Animation and Games," "C# Programming for SMA/SMK and Students," "MATLAB For Students and Researchers," "Graphics in JavaScript: Quick Learning Series," "JavaScript Image Processing Methods: From A to Z," "Java GUI Case Study: AWT & Swing," "Basic CSS and JavaScript," "PHP/MySQL Programming: Cookbook," "Visual Basic: Cookbook," "C++ Programming for High Schools/Vocational Schools and Students," "Concepts and Practices of C++," "PHP/MySQL For Students," "C# Programming: From A to Z," "Visual Basic for SMA/SMK and Students," and "C# .NET and SQL Server for High School/Vocational School and Students." Furthermore, at the ANDI Yogyakarta publisher, Vivian Siahaan has contributed to several notable books, including "Python Programming Theory and Practice," "Python GUI Programming," "Python GUI and Database," "Build From Zero School Database Management System In Python/MySQL," "Database Management System in Python/MySQL," "Python/MySQL For Management Systems of Criminal Track Record Database," "Java/MySQL For Management Systems of Criminal Track Records Database," "Database and Cryptography Using Java/MySQL," and "Build From Zero School Database Management System With Java/MySQL." Vivian's diverse range of expertise in programming languages, combined with her passion for exploring new horizons, makes her a dynamic and versatile individual in the field of technology. Her dedication to learning, coupled with her strong analytical and problem-solving skills, positions her as a valuable asset in any programming endeavor. Vivian Siahaan's contributions to the world of programming and literature continue to inspire and empower aspiring programmers and readers alike.

Rismon Hasiholan Sianipar, born in Pematang Siantar in 1994, is a distinguished researcher and expert in the field of electrical engineering. After completing his education at SMAN 3 Pematang Siantar, Rismon ventured to the city of Jogjakarta to pursue his academic journey. He obtained his Bachelor of Engineering (S.T) and Master of Engineering (M.T) degrees in Electrical Engineering from Gadjah Mada University in 1998 and 2001, respectively, under the guidance of esteemed professors, Dr. Adhi Soesanto and Dr. Thomas Sri Widodo. During his studies, Rismon focused on researching non-stationary signals and their energy analysis using time-frequency maps. He explored the dynamic nature of signal energy distribution on time-frequency maps and developed innovative techniques using discrete wavelet transformations to design non-linear filters for data pattern analysis. His research showcased the application of these techniques in various fields. In recognition of his academic prowess, Rismon was awarded the prestigious Monbukagakusho scholarship by the Japanese Government in 2003. He went on to pursue his Master of Engineering (M.Eng) and Doctor of Engineering (Dr.Eng) degrees at Yamaguchi University, supervised by Prof. Dr. Hidetoshi Miike. Rismon's master's and doctoral theses revolved around combining the SR-FHN (Stochastic Resonance Fitzhugh-Nagumo) filter strength with the cryptosystem ECC (elliptic curve cryptography) 4096-bit. This innovative approach effectively suppressed noise in digital images and videos while ensuring their authenticity. Rismon's research findings have been published in renowned international scientific journals, and his patents have been officially registered in Japan. Notably, one of his patents, with registration number 2008-009549, gained recognition. He actively collaborates with several universities and research institutions in Japan, specializing in cryptography, cryptanalysis, and digital forensics, particularly in the areas of audio, image, and video analysis. With a passion for knowledge sharing, Rismon has authored numerous national and international scientific articles and authored several national books. He has also actively participated in workshops related to cryptography, cryptanalysis, digital watermarking, and digital forensics. During these workshops, Rismon has assisted Prof. Hidetoshi Miike in developing applications related to digital image and video processing, steganography, cryptography, watermarking, and more, which serve as valuable training materials. Rismon's field of interest encompasses multimedia security, signal processing, digital image and video analysis, cryptography, digital communication, digital forensics, and data compression. He continues to advance his research by developing applications using programming languages such as Python, MATLAB, C++, C, VB.NET, C#.NET, R, and Java. These applications serve both research and commercial purposes, further contributing to the advancement of signal and image analysis. Rismon Hasiholan Sianipar is a dedicated researcher and expert in the field of electrical engineering, particularly in the areas of signal processing, cryptography, and digital forensics. His academic achievements, patented inventions, and extensive publications demonstrate his commitment to advancing knowledge in these fields. Rismon's contributions to academia and his collaborations with prestigious institutions in Japan have solidified his position as a respected figure in the scientific community. Through his ongoing research and development of innovative applications, Rismon continues to make significant contributions to the field of electrical engineering.

ABOUT THE BOOK

The first project, frame_differencing.py, integrates motion detection within video sequences using a graphical user interface (GUI) facilitated by Tkinter, enhanced by image processing capabilities from OpenCV, and image handling using PIL. The core functionality, embedded in the FrameDifferencer class, organizes the application structure starting from initialization, which sets up the GUI layout with video control widgets, playback features, and filter selection. The script processes video frames to detect motion through grayscale conversion, Gaussian blurring, and frame differencing, highlighting motion by thresholding and contour detection. Enhanced interactivity is provided through real-time updates of motion detections on the GUI and user-enabled area selection for detailed analysis, including color histogram display. This flexible and extensible tool supports various applications from security surveillance to educational uses in image processing, embodying a practical approach to video analysis.

The second project RunningGaussianAverage utilizes the running Gaussian average technique for motion detection within a graphical user interface (GUI) built on Tkinter. Upon initialization, it configures a master window and sets up video processing capabilities, including video stream handling, frame analysis, and displaying results on the GUI. The interface includes playback controls, a video display canvas, and a listbox for motion event notifications, allowing interactive management of video analysis. Core functionalities like video loading, playback control, and frame processing leverage the imageio and OpenCV libraries to handle video input and perform real-time image processing tasks such as blurring, grayscale conversion, and motion detection through frame differencing. The application is structured to provide an intuitive platform for users to engage with motion detection technology effectively, showcasing changes directly within the GUI.

The third project introduces a sophisticated application that utilizes the Mixture of Gaussians (MOG) method for motion detection within a user-friendly Tkinter-based GUI. Leveraging OpenCV's cv2.createBackgroundSubtractorMOG2(), the application excels in background modeling and foreground detection, effectively handling various lighting conditions and shadow detection, making it ideal for security and surveillance applications. The GUI is designed to enhance user interaction, featuring video display, playback controls, adjustable detection settings, and dynamic results display through list boxes and scrollbars. It also offers advanced filtering options like Gaussian and median blurs, along with more complex filters such as wavelet transforms and anisotropic diffusion, all adjustable via the GUI. This setup allows for real-time frame processing, detection visualization, and interactive exploration, making it a potent tool for educational purposes, professional security setups, and enthusiasts in video processing technology.

The fourth project develops a sophisticated motion detection system using Kernel Density Estimation (KDE), integrated into a Tkinter-based graphical interface, simplifying the advanced image processing for users without deep technical expertise. Central to this application is the use of OpenCV's MOG2 background subtractor which excels in differentiating foreground activity from the background, especially in varied lighting and shadow conditions, thus enhancing robustness in diverse environments. The GUI is intuitively designed, featuring video playback controls and real-time video frame rendering along with a motion density map that accumulates and visualizes movement patterns over time. The application processes video frames by applying Gaussian blurring to reduce noise and then uses the MOG2 model to create a foreground mask, refined further to delineate motion clearly. This setup allows for precise contour detection to identify and mark moving objects, providing detailed motion event analysis directly on the interface. This project effectively marries complex image processing capabilities with a user-friendly interface, making sophisticated motion detection technology accessible for surveillance, research, and broader applications.

The fifth project develops an advanced motion detection system using the K-Nearest Neighbors (KNN) algorithm for effective background subtraction, all within a user-friendly Tkinter-based graphical interface, ideal for surveillance and monitoring applications. The KNN background subtractor stands out for its dynamic adaptation, enhancing detection accuracy under varying lighting conditions while minimizing false positives from environmental changes. Users interact through a thoughtfully designed GUI, featuring real-time video playback, motion event logs, and intuitive controls like play, pause, and frame navigation. Additionally, the system includes various filters such as Gaussian blur and wavelet transforms to optimize detection quality. Detected motions are highlighted with bounding boxes and detailed in a sidebar, simplifying the tracking process. Advanced features like zoom and area-specific analysis further augment the tool's utility, making it versatile for applications ranging from security surveillance to traffic monitoring, all the while maintaining ease of use and robust analytical capabilities.

The sixth project, "Median Filtering with Filtering", develops a sophisticated motion detection application using Python, integrating Tkinter for the GUI, OpenCV for image processing, and ImageIO for video management. This application utilizes median filtering to effectively reduce noise in video frames, enhancing motion detection capabilities for security surveillance, wildlife monitoring, and other applications requiring movement tracking. The GUI is intuitively designed with video playback controls, adjustable motion detection sensitivity, and a log of detected movements, making it highly interactive and user-friendly. Users can also apply various filters like Gaussian and bilateral smoothing to improve image quality under different conditions. The application is built with expandability in mind, allowing for easy integration of additional filters, enhanced algorithms, or more sophisticated functionalities to meet specific user needs or to be incorporated into larger systems.

CONTENT

MOTION DETECTION WITH FRAME DIFFERENCING — 1
DESCRIPTION — 1
IMPORTING LIBRARIES — 4
CLASS AND CONSTRUCTOR — 6
CREATING WIDGETS — 8
UPDATING THRESHOLD — 12
CONTROLLING VIDEO PLAYBACK — 14
PROCESSING FRAME — 17
DISPLAYING FRAME — 20
INTEGRATION OF PROCESSING AND DISPLAYING FRAME — 23
NAVIGATING FRAME — 25
UPDATING CURRENT FRAME INDEX — 28
HANDLING MOUSE EVENTS — 30
ANALYZING HISTOGRAM — 33
CREATINNG POPUP WINDOW — 36
DISPLAYING HISTOGRAM OF CROPPED IMAGE — 39
HANDLING IMAGE FILTERING — 44
DEFINING FILTERS — 48
ENTRY POINT FOR APPLICATION — 53
RUNNING PROGRAM — 55
SOURCE CODE — 57

MOTION DETECTION WITH RUNNING GAUSSIAN AVERAGE — 70
DESCRIPTION — 70
PROCESSING FRAME — 72
RUNNING PROGRAM — 75
SOURCE CODE — 77

MOTION DETECTION WITH MIXTURE OF GAUSSIANS (MOG) — 91
DESCRIPTION — 91
PROCESSING FRAME — 93

RUNNING PROGRAM	96
SOURCE CODE	98

MOTION DETECTION WITH KERNEL DENSITY ESTIMATION — **111**

DESCRIPTION	111
PROCESSING FRAME	113
RUNNING PROGRAM	116
SOURCE CODE	118

MOTION DETECTION WITH K-NEAREST NEIGHBORS (KNN) — **132**

DESCRIPTION	132
PROCESSING FRAME	134
RUNNING PROGRAM	136
SOURCE CODE	139

MOTION DETECTION WITH MEDIAN FILTERING — **152**

DESCRIPTION	152
PROCESSING FRAME	154
RUNNING PROGRAM	157
SOURCE CODE	158

Bibliography — **172**

MOTION DETECTION WITH FRAME DIFFERENCING

DESCRIPTION

The project titled frame_differencing.py is designed to facilitate motion detection through frame differencing in video sequences, providing a graphical user interface (GUI) with various controls and visualization options. This utility leverages libraries like Tkinter for the GUI, OpenCV for image processing, and PIL for image handling.

Structure and Initialization

The core of the script is encapsulated in the FrameDifferencer class, which initializes the main window, video playback controls, and various interactive elements for user input. The class constructor sets up the application window and calls create_widgets to populate the GUI with video control buttons, a video frame display canvas, a listbox for displaying motion detections, and entry fields for parameters like the threshold for motion detection.

GUI Layout and Widgets

The create_widgets function organizes the GUI into sections with a display frame for the video output and a control panel containing buttons to open, play, pause, stop, navigate through frames, and adjust settings like the threshold for motion detection. Additionally, it includes a combobox for selecting various image processing filters to apply to the video frames.

Video Handling

The application provides functionality to open video files through a file dialog. It supports playing, pausing, and stopping video playback. The video frames are processed on the fly to detect motion by comparing the current frame with the previous one, identifying differences above a specified threshold.

Frame Processing

The process_frame() method is a critical part of the application where frame differencing occurs. It converts frames to grayscale, applies Gaussian blurring to reduce noise, and computes the absolute difference between the current and the previous frame. A binary threshold is then applied to this difference to isolate regions of significant change, which are interpreted as motion. Detected motion regions are contoured, and bounding boxes are drawn around these areas.

Display Functions

The application updates the GUI to display the processed frames and motion detections. The listbox is updated dynamically to list the centers of detected motion areas. The display_frame() function handles rendering of the current video frame on the canvas.

Additional Interactive Features

The script includes interactive capabilities such as mouse event handling to zoom and navigate within the video frame, drag to define areas for more detailed analysis, and display histograms of color distributions within selected regions.

Filtering Options

The application allows the user to apply various filters to the video frames, selectable via a combobox. These filters include Gaussian blur, median blur, and more sophisticated options like bilateral filtering and wavelet transforms. This feature is crucial for experimenting with different preprocessing techniques to enhance motion detection accuracy or explore different image characteristics.

Analysis Tools

Upon selecting a region in the video frame, users can invoke the analyze_histogram method to open a new window displaying the cropped region and its color histograms. This feature aids in detailed analysis of specific areas within the video, useful for tasks such as surveillance where understanding the color and intensity distribution within a motion region can be crucial.

Extensibility

The code structure allows for easy expansion and customization. New filters and features can be integrated by extending the existing framework, making it a versatile tool for various applications beyond simple motion detection, such as object tracking, security surveillance, and educational purposes in image processing.

Execution

Finally, the script contains a main block that initializes the Tkinter root widget and starts the GUI application, making it standalone and executable. This design encapsulates the functionality within the FrameDifferencer class, allowing it to be potentially integrated into larger systems or applications as a module.

In summary, frame_differencing.py serves as a comprehensive tool for motion detection in video streams, equipped with interactive GUI features, advanced image processing capabilities, and extensible architecture suitable for various real-world applications.

IMPORTING LIBRARIES

```
import tkinter as tk
from tkinter import ttk
from tkinter import filedialog
from PIL import Image, ImageTk
import cv2
import imageio
import matplotlib.pyplot as plt
import pywt
import numpy as np
```

The code snippet shows the import statements for a variety of libraries used to create a graphical user interface and process images and videos. Here's a breakdown of what each imported library does and its role in a potential application:

- tkinter: This is the standard Python interface to the Tk GUI toolkit. It is widely used for creating graphical user interfaces (GUIs) due to its simplicity and availability as part of the Python standard library. It provides various widgets including buttons, menus, text fields, labels, and more, which can be used to build user interfaces.
- ttk: The themed Tkinter (ttk) module provides access to the Tk themed widget set, which allows for a more modern and stylish appearance of the GUI components compared to the classic Tk widgets. ttk stands for "themed tk," offering themes that can change the look of standard widgets while keeping the same functionality.

- filedialog: This module from Tkinter provides classes and factory functions for creating file/directory selection windows. It allows users to open or save files via a dialog box, which is extremely useful in applications that require input data from files, such as image or video files.
- Image, ImageTk: Part of the Python Imaging Library (PIL), which is now known as Pillow. Image provides a class with the same name which is used to represent a PIL image. The module supports opening, manipulating, and saving many different image file formats. ImageTk is used to interface between PIL images and Tkinter widgets. It is specifically used to convert images from PIL formats to formats that Tkinter can use on labels, buttons, canvases, and other widgets.
- cv2: OpenCV (Open Source Computer Vision Library) is an open-source computer vision and machine learning software library. cv2 is the Python package that interfaces with this library. It is crucial for image and video analysis, capable of tasks such as reading and writing images and videos, processing images (filters, transformations), and performing complex vision tasks like face recognition and object detection.
- imageio: This library provides an easy interface to read and write a wide range of image data, including animated images, video streams, and volumetric data. Unlike cv2, which primarily focuses on real-time computer vision, imageio is designed for easy reading and writing of data in common storage formats.
- plt: Part of the matplotlib library, plt is used for creating static, interactive, and animated visualizations in Python. In the context of an application that involves image and video processing, plt could be used to display histograms, plots, and other types of visual data analysis.
- pywt: PyWavelets, or pywt, is a library for wavelet transforms in Python, which are mathematical functions useful in digital signal processing and image compression. Using wavelet transform, the library can analyze and process signals and images at multiple scales or resolutions.

- np: NumPy is the fundamental package for scientific computing with Python. It provides support for large, multi-dimensional arrays and matrices, along with a large collection of high-level mathematical functions to operate on these arrays. In image processing, NumPy arrays are often used to store and manipulate pixel data.

These imports are aimed at handling, processing, and analyzing images and videos, possibly incorporating GUI elements for user interaction and visualization.

CLASS AND CONSTRUCTOR

```
class FrameDifferencer:
    def __init__(self, master):
        self.master = master
        self.master.title("Motion Detection with Frame Differencing")
        self.bbox_rect = None  # Initialize bbox_rect attribute to None

        # Video related variables
        self.video = None
        self.previous_frame = None
        self.frame_index = 0
        self.paused = True
        self.threshold = 5  # Default threshold for frame differencing

        # Creates widgets
        self.create_widgets(master)
```

The code defines the constructor (__init__) of a Python class named FrameDifferencer. This class appears to be designed for creating a graphical user interface (GUI) application that detects motion in video streams using frame differencing. Here's a detailed explanation of each part of the constructor and its role in the application:

Initialization of FrameDifferencer class

master: The master parameter is expected to be a Tkinter widget (commonly the main window tk.Tk()), which acts as the parent widget for all other GUI components. This is a standard approach in Tkinter applications, where a "master" or "root" widget serves as the container for the application.

Setting the Application Title

self.master.title("Motion Detection with Frame Differencing"): This line sets the title of the main window of the GUI to "Motion Detection with Frame Differencing". It helps users identify the purpose of the application.

Variable Initialization

- self.bbox_rect = None: Initializes bbox_rect to None. This variable will be used later to store a reference to a bounding box rectangle drawn on the video display, possibly indicating areas of motion or regions of interest.
- self.video = None: This initializes self.video as None, which will later hold the video stream or file for processing.
- self.previous_frame = None: Similar to self.video, this variable is initialized as None and will store the previous video frame to be used in frame differencing.
- self.frame_index = 0: This counter tracks the current frame number in the video stream. Starting at 0, it likely gets incremented as the video plays.
- self.paused = True: A boolean flag initialized as True, indicating that video playback starts in a paused state. It controls the play/pause status of the video.
- self.threshold = 5: Sets the default threshold for motion detection to 5. This threshold could be used in processing the video frames to determine the level of change that constitutes motion.

Widget Creation

self.create_widgets(master): This method call is responsible for setting up the user interface elements. Although the actual method is not shown in the snippet, typically, create_widgets would create various widgets like buttons, sliders, labels, and display areas. These widgets are used for interactions such as starting/pausing video playback, adjusting settings, and displaying video frames.

Summary

The constructor of FrameDifferencer sets up the initial state of the application, preparing variables and GUI components for functionality that will be added in other methods of the class. The setup suggests that the application will involve interactive video playback with tools to detect and possibly analyze motion between frames, using techniques like frame differencing where the absolute difference between two consecutive frames is used to detect changes (motion) in the scene.

CREATING WIDGETS

```python
def create_widgets(self, master):
    # Create a frame for the canvas and listbox
    display_frame = tk.Frame(master)
    display_frame.pack(fill=tk.BOTH, expand=True)

    # Set up the canvas
    self.canvas = tk.Canvas(display_frame, width=800, height=600)
    self.canvas.pack(side=tk.LEFT, fill=tk.BOTH, expand=True)
    self.canvas.bind("<MouseWheel>", self.on_mousewheel)
    self.canvas.bind("<ButtonPress-1>", self.on_press)
    self.canvas.bind("<B1-Motion>", self.on_drag)
    self.canvas.bind("<ButtonRelease-1>", self.on_release)  # Bind ButtonRelease event

    # Set up the listbox for displaying centers
    self.listbox = tk.Listbox(display_frame, width=40, height=20)
    self.listbox.pack(side=tk.RIGHT, fill=tk.Y)

    # Add scrollbar to the listbox
    scrollbar = tk.Scrollbar(display_frame, orient="vertical", command=self.listbox.yview)
    scrollbar.pack(side=tk.RIGHT, fill=tk.Y)
```

```python
        self.listbox.config(yscrollcommand=scrollbar.set)

        # Control Panel below the display frame
        control_panel = tk.Frame(master)
        control_panel.pack(fill=tk.X)

        self.open_button = tk.Button(control_panel, text="Open Video", command=self.open_video)
        self.open_button.pack(side=tk.LEFT)

        self.play_button = tk.Button(control_panel, text="Play/Pause", command=self.toggle_play_pause)
        self.play_button.pack(side=tk.LEFT)

        self.stop_button = tk.Button(control_panel, text="Stop", command=self.stop_video)
        self.stop_button.pack(side=tk.LEFT)

        self.prev_button = tk.Button(control_panel, text="Previous Frame", command=self.prev_frame)
        self.prev_button.pack(side=tk.LEFT)

        self.next_button = tk.Button(control_panel, text="Next Frame", command=self.next_frame)
        self.next_button.pack(side=tk.LEFT)

        # Frame number label
        self.frame_label = tk.Label(master, text="Frame: 0", font=('Helvetica', 18))
        self.frame_label.pack()

        # Threshold Control
        self.threshold_label = tk.Label(control_panel, text="Threshold:")
        self.threshold_label.pack(side=tk.LEFT)

        self.threshold_entry = tk.Entry(control_panel, width=5)
        self.threshold_entry.pack(side=tk.LEFT)
        self.threshold_entry.insert(0, '5')  # Default threshold value
        self.threshold_entry.bind("<Return>", self.update_threshold)

        # Available filters
        self.filters = ["None", "Gaussian", "Mean", "Median", "Bilateral Filtering",
                    "Non-local Means Denoising", "Anisotropic Diffusion",
                    "Total Variation Denoising", "Wiener Filter",
                    "Adaptive Thresholding", "Haar Wavelet Transform",
                    "Daubechies Wavelet Transform"]

        # Subframe for complex controls such as combobox
        filter_frame = tk.Frame(control_panel)
```

```
filter_frame.pack(side=tk.LEFT, fill=tk.X, expand=True)

# Combobox for Selecting Filters
self.filter_combobox = ttk.Combobox(filter_frame, values=self.filters)
self.filter_combobox.pack(side=tk.LEFT, padx=10, pady=5)
self.filter_combobox.current(0)  # Set default value
```

The create_widgets() method within the FrameDifferencer class systematically establishes the graphical user interface (GUI) components for the motion detection application. This method orchestrates the layout and the functional elements of the GUI, enabling user interaction and the display of video data. Here's a breakdown of each component and their role:

Display Frame Setup
- Display Frame: A tk.Frame called display_frame is created and packed into the master widget using fill=tk.BOTH and expand=True to utilize the maximum available space. This frame serves as a container for the canvas and the listbox.
- Canvas: A tk.Canvas is set up within display_frame with specific dimensions (800x600 pixels). This canvas is where the video frames will be displayed. Event bindings (<MouseWheel>, <ButtonPress-1>, <B1-Motion>, <ButtonRelease-1>) are added to handle zooming, pressing, dragging, and releasing actions, enabling interactive features like adjusting the view or selecting regions within the video frames.
- Listbox with Scrollbar: Positioned next to the canvas, this tk.Listbox displays motion detection data (like the centers of detected motion regions). It is equipped with a vertical scrollbar to handle overflow, allowing users to navigate through a potentially long list of detected motions.

Control Panel Setup

- Control Panel: This tk.Frame houses several operational buttons (Open Video, Play/Pause, Stop, Previous Frame, Next Frame) and other control elements. It is packed with fill=tk.X to extend across the window horizontally.
- Buttons: Each button is linked to a specific functionality:
  - Open Video: Opens a file dialog to load a video.
  - Play/Pause: Toggles between playing and pausing the video.
  - Stop: Stops the video playback and resets the frame index.
  - Previous Frame, Next Frame: Navigate through the video frames one by one.
- Frame Label: Displays the current frame number, aiding in navigation and reference during video analysis.

Threshold Control

Threshold Label and Entry: A label and an entry widget allow the user to input and update the threshold value used for detecting motion. The value can be submitted by pressing the "Return" key, which triggers update_threshold to adjust the motion detection sensitivity.

Filtering Options

- Filters: A list of string values representing different image processing filters that can be applied to the video frames. These include basic filters like Gaussian blur and more advanced techniques like wavelet transforms.
- Filter Combobox: A ttk.Combobox allows the user to select from the available filters. It's initialized with the filters list and set to a default value ("None").

Layout Considerations

Geometry Management: The use of pack() with directions (side=tk.LEFT, side=tk.RIGHT, etc.) and options like fill and expand in various widgets helps in organizing the layout in a clear and functional manner, ensuring that all components are accessible and visually integrated.

Summary

The create_widgets() method effectively sets up the user interface for a video processing application, providing tools for interaction, video manipulation, and visualization. It facilitates user engagement through control elements while ensuring that video analysis tasks like motion detection and filtering are user-configurable and interactive. The method lays a solid foundation for the rest of the application's functionality, which would be implemented in other methods and event handlers of the FrameDifferencer class.

UPDATING THRESHOLD

```python
def update_threshold(self, event):
    try:
        self.threshold = int(self.threshold_entry.get())
        print(f"Threshold updated to {self.threshold}")
    except ValueError:
        print("Invalid input for threshold. Please enter an integer.")
```

The update_threshold() method in the FrameDifferencer class is designed to handle updates to the motion detection threshold value based on user input from the GUI. Here's a breakdown of how this method functions:

Method Definition and Purpose

Purpose: This method updates the threshold used for detecting motion in the video frames. The threshold is a critical parameter that determines how sensitive the motion detection algorithm is to changes between frames. A lower threshold may detect more minor movements, while a higher threshold might only react to more significant changes.

Execution Flow

Event Parameter: The method takes a single parameter, event, which is automatically passed by Tkinter when the method is bound to an event like pressing the "Return" key in the threshold entry box. This setup allows for real-time updates of the threshold value as soon as the user submits their input.

Try-Except Block:

- Try Block: The method attempts to convert the string value retrieved from self.threshold_entry.get() to an integer. If successful, it updates self.threshold with the new integer value. This value is then printed to the console with the message Threshold updated to {self.threshold}, providing immediate feedback to the user about the successful update.

- Except Block: If the conversion fails (typically because the input is not a valid integer), a ValueError is raised. The method catches this exception and prints an error message (Invalid input for threshold. Please enter an integer.) to the console. This message guides the user to correct their input, ensuring the program remains robust against invalid data entries.

Practical Use

- User Interaction: This method directly involves the user in tuning the motion detection functionality. By allowing the threshold to be set interactively, users can experiment with different settings to achieve the best results based on the specific conditions in the video (e.g., lighting conditions, the scale of motion to be detected).

- Feedback Mechanism: The immediate feedback provided via console messages helps users understand the effect of their adjustments and correct any errors in real-time, enhancing the usability and responsiveness of the application.

Summary

The update_threshold() method exemplifies a simple yet effective approach to handling user input and updating key parameters in a real-time application. It enhances the application's interactivity and allows for flexible adjustment of its core functionality, which is critical in tasks like motion detection where the optimal settings may vary significantly between different videos or environments. This method thus plays a crucial role in the application's overall performance and user experience.

CONTROLLING VIDEO PLAYBACK

```python
def open_video(self):
    video_path = filedialog.askopenfilename(filetypes=[("Video files", "*.mp4;*.avi;*.mkv;*.wmv")])
    if video_path:
        self.video = imageio.get_reader(video_path)
        self.frame_index = 0
        self.previous_frame = None
        self.paused = False
        self.play_video()
        self.update_frame_label()

def toggle_play_pause(self):
    self.paused = not self.paused
    if not self.paused:
        self.play_video()

def stop_video(self):
    self.paused = True
    self.frame_index = 0
    self.previous_frame = None
    self.update_frame_label()
    self.display_frame(None)  # Clear the canvas

def play_video(self):
    if not self.paused and self.video:
        if self.frame_index < len(self.video):
            try:
                frame_data = self.video.get_data(self.frame_index)
                frame = cv2.cvtColor(frame_data, cv2.COLOR_RGB2BGR)
```

```
            self.process_frame(frame)
            self.frame_index += 1
            self.master.after(42, self.play_video)  # Schedule next frame
    except IndexError:
        print("Reached the end of the video.")
        self.paused = True  # Stop the video playback
    self.update_frame_label()
```

The open_video(), toggle_play_pause(), stop_video(), and play_video() methods in FrameDifferencer class collectively manage the video playback functionality in application. Here's a detailed overview of how each method operates and integrates with the GUI and other components:

open_video() Method

- Functionality: This method allows the user to open a video file via a file dialog. It supports various file types including MP4, AVI, MKV, and WMV.
- Implementation:
    - File Dialog: Opens a dialog box allowing the user to select a video file.
    - Video Initialization: If a file is chosen, the method initializes the video stream using imageio.get_reader(video_path), resets the frame_index and previous_frame, and sets paused to False to start playing the video automatically.
    - Playback Trigger: Calls self.play_video() to start the video playback and updates the frame label using self.update_frame_label().

toggle_play_pause() Method

- Functionality: Toggles the playback state of the video between play and pause.
- Implementation:
    - Toggle State: Flips the paused boolean attribute. If paused becomes False, it calls self.play_video() to resume video playback.

stop_video() Method
- Functionality: Stops the video playback and resets the video to the beginning.
- Implementation:
  - Stop and Reset: Sets paused to True, resets frame_index to 0, and clears previous_frame.
  - GUI Update: Calls self.update_frame_label() to update the frame number display and self.display_frame(None) to clear the canvas, effectively removing any currently displayed video frame.

play_video() Method
- Functionality: Handles the actual video frame fetching and processing in a loop until the video is paused or ends.
- Implementation:
  - Frame Processing: While not paused and there are more frames, it retrieves each frame using self.video.get_data(self.frame_index), converts it to the BGR color space (required for OpenCV operations), and processes it using self.process_frame(frame).
  - Frame Advancement: Increments frame_index and schedules the next frame to be processed after a short delay (42 ms, roughly corresponding to 24 FPS) using self.master.after(42, self.play_video).
  - End of Video: Checks if the current frame index exceeds the number of frames in the video and stops playback if it does, updating the GUI to reflect this.

Integration and Error Handling
These methods work together to control video playback seamlessly, allowing for interactive control over the video with play, pause, and stop functionalities.

Error handling is implemented in play_video to catch IndexError, which may occur if the frame index exceeds the available number of frames, indicating the video has ended.

Summary

The video management methods in FrameDifferencer are critical for providing a responsive and user-friendly interface for video playback in an application designed for motion detection. They handle the complexities of video file operations, user interactions for controlling playback, and real-time processing of video frames, which is essential for the core functionality of motion detection through frame differencing. These methods ensure that users can easily load, view, and control their video data while interacting with the motion detection features of the application.

PROCESSING FRAME

```python
def process_frame(self, frame):
    gray = cv2.cvtColor(frame, cv2.COLOR_BGR2GRAY)
    gray = cv2.GaussianBlur(gray, (21, 21), 0)
    if self.previous_frame is None:
        self.previous_frame = gray
        return

    frame_delta = cv2.absdiff(self.previous_frame, gray)
    thresh = cv2.threshold(frame_delta, self.threshold, 255, cv2.THRESH_BINARY)[1]
    thresh = cv2.dilate(thresh, None, iterations=2)
    contours, _ = cv2.findContours(thresh.copy(), cv2.RETR_EXTERNAL, cv2.CHAIN_APPROX_SIMPLE)

    self.listbox.delete(0, tk.END)  # Clear existing entries in the listbox
    box_number = 0  # Initialize box number
    for contour in contours:
        if cv2.contourArea(contour) < 500:
            continue
        box_number += 1  # Increment the box number for each contour
        (x, y, w, h) = cv2.boundingRect(contour)
        center_x, center_y = x + w // 2, y + h // 2
```

```
        self.listbox.insert(tk.END, f"Box {box_number}: Center ({center_x},
{center_y})")
        cv2.rectangle(frame, (x, y), (x+w, y+h), (50, 0, 255), 2)
        cv2.putText(frame, f"{box_number}", (x + 5, y + 20),
cv2.FONT_HERSHEY_SIMPLEX, 0.6, (0, 255, 0), 2)

    self.display_frame(frame)
    self.previous_frame = gray
```

The process_frame() method in FrameDifferencer class is key to performing motion detection via frame differencing in video streams. Here's an analysis of its functionality, step-by-step:

Method Overview

This method processes individual frames of the video to detect significant movements by comparing the current frame with the previous frame. It performs several image processing operations to achieve this:

Step-by-Step Processing

1. Grayscale Conversion:

    Converts the input frame from BGR to grayscale. Grayscale conversion is a common preliminary step in motion detection because it simplifies the data by removing color information, focusing on intensity values which are sufficient for detecting motion.

2. Gaussian Blurring:

    Applies Gaussian blur to the grayscale image ((21, 21) is the kernel size, and 0 is the standard deviation). Blurring helps reduce image noise which can lead to false detections. It also smooths out the edges which simplifies the calculation of differences between frames.

3. Frame Initialization:

Checks if self.previous_frame is None (which it will be on the first run), and if so, sets self.previous_frame to the current gray frame and exits the method. This setup step ensures that there is a previous frame to compare against in subsequent calls.

4. Frame Differencing:

    Calculates the absolute difference between the current blurred grayscale frame and the previous blurred grayscale frame stored in self.previous_frame. This difference highlights areas of significant change between the two frames.

5. Thresholding:

    Applies a binary threshold to the frame difference. Pixels with differences greater than the specified self.threshold are set to 255 (white), and all others are set to 0 (black). This creates a binary image where white areas represent significant movements.

6. Dilation:

    Dilates the thresholded image to enhance the white areas. This step helps fill in gaps and strengthen the white regions corresponding to movements, making it easier to detect and contour these areas.

7. Contour Detection:

    Finds contours in the dilated binary image using cv2.findContours. Contours are used to outline the white patches, which represent movements.

Motion Detection and Annotation

The method then iterates over each detected contour:

- Area Filtering: Skips contours smaller than 500 pixels to avoid noise and small irrelevant movements.
- Bounding Box Calculation: For each significant contour, calculates the bounding box and derives the center of the box.
- Listbox Update: Adds the center coordinates of each significant motion to the listbox in the GUI.

- Drawing on Frame: Draws rectangles and labels around the detected motion areas directly on the frame for visual feedback.

Final Steps

Display and Update:

- Calls self.display_frame(frame) to update the GUI display with the annotated frame showing detected movements.
- Updates self.previous_frame with the current gray frame, preparing it for the next frame's processing.

Summary

The process_frame() method effectively identifies and visualizes motion between video frames, utilizing classic computer vision techniques like frame differencing, thresholding, and contour detection. This method is central to the functionality of the FrameDifferencer application, enabling it to monitor and highlight areas of activity within the video, which can be crucial for security systems, automated monitoring, and various other applications in motion analysis.

DISPLAYING FRAME

```
def display_frame(self, frame):
    if frame is not None:
        image = cv2.cvtColor(frame, cv2.COLOR_BGR2RGB)
        image = Image.fromarray(image)
        photo = ImageTk.PhotoImage(image=image)
        self.canvas.create_image(0, 0, anchor=tk.NW, image=photo)
        self.canvas.image = photo  # Keep the reference
    else:
        self.canvas.delete("all")
```

The display_frame() method in the FrameDifferencer class plays a crucial role in visualizing the video frames processed by the application, especially after applying operations such as motion detection. This method ensures that each frame, potentially with annotations like motion contours, is displayed to the user via a Tkinter canvas. Here's a detailed breakdown of how this method works:

Method Functionality

Purpose: To display a given frame (which can be a raw or processed video frame) on a Tkinter canvas widget. If no frame is provided (i.e., frame is None), it clears the canvas.

Processing Steps

1. Frame Check:

    The method first checks if a frame is provided (if frame is not None:). If there is no frame (i.e., frame is None), the method proceeds to clear the canvas using self.canvas.delete("all"). This is useful for cases like stopping the video where you might want to reset the display.

2. Color Space Conversion:

    If a frame is provided, it converts the frame from BGR (Blue, Green, Red - the color format used by OpenCV) to RGB (Red, Green, Blue - the color format used by most image display libraries including Tkinter). This conversion is necessary because the frame processing in OpenCV typically outputs in BGR format, but graphical display libraries and standards generally use RGB.

3. Creating Image Object:

    Uses Image.fromarray to convert the NumPy array (the image data format used by OpenCV) into a PIL Image object. PIL (Python Imaging Library, now known as Pillow) acts as a bridge between image processing with OpenCV and displaying images in Tkinter.

4. Creating PhotoImage Object:

Converts the PIL Image object into a ImageTk.PhotoImage object. This is the format required by Tkinter for displaying images on widgets like Canvas.
5. Updating the Canvas:
    - Uses self.canvas.create_image(0, 0, anchor=tk.NW, image=photo) to display the image on the canvas. The image is anchored at the northwest corner (anchor=tk.NW) of the canvas. This ensures the image fills the canvas starting from the top-left corner.
    - It's important to store a reference to the PhotoImage object in the canvas widget (self.canvas.image = photo). This is necessary because Tkinter does not keep a reference to the image object itself. Without this reference, the Python garbage collector would remove the PhotoImage object, and the image would not display or disappear from the canvas.

Summary

The display_frame() method encapsulates the process of displaying video frames on a GUI, handling necessary format conversions and updating the canvas. By maintaining the correct sequence of operations and ensuring format compatibility, this method seamlessly integrates the image processing backend with the frontend display, essential for any GUI-based video processing application. This method effectively bridges the gap between the raw frame processing done with OpenCV and the user interface managed with Tkinter, making it a key component in the visualization of video data and results in the FrameDifferencer application.

INTEGRATION OF PROCESSING AND DISPLAYING FRAME

```python
def process_and_display_frame(self):
    if self.video and self.frame_index >= 0 and self.frame_index < len(self.video):
        try:
            frame_data = self.video.get_data(self.frame_index)
            frame = cv2.cvtColor(frame_data, cv2.COLOR_RGB2BGR)
            self.process_frame(frame)
        except IndexError:
            print(f"Frame index {self.frame_index} is out of range.")
            self.paused = True  # Pause to prevent further errors
        except Exception as e:
            print(f"Error processing frame: {e}")
            self.paused = True
    self.update_frame_label()
```

The process_and_display_frame() method in FrameDifferencer class is a crucial function that integrates several key aspects of video processing and display. This method specifically handles fetching, processing, and ensuring the proper display of individual video frames. Here's a detailed walkthrough of its implementation and functionality:

Method Purpose
- Primary Goal: To fetch a frame from the video based on the current frame_index, process this frame for motion detection, and update the GUI to reflect changes.
- Error Handling: Includes robust error checking to gracefully manage cases where the frame index is out of the expected range or other unexpected errors occur during frame processing.

Step-by-Step Execution
1. Video and Frame Index Validation:

   The method first checks if self.video is valid and if self.frame_index is within the allowable range (from 0 up to but not including len(self.video)). This ensures that there is a video loaded and the frame index points to an existing frame within the video.

2. Frame Retrieval and Conversion:
   - Frame Data Retrieval: Retrieves frame data using self.video.get_data(self.frame_index), which extracts the frame from the video at the specified index.
   - Color Space Conversion: Converts the frame from RGB (used by imageio library) to BGR color space because OpenCV functions primarily operate in BGR. This step is crucial for subsequent image processing operations which rely on OpenCV.

3. Frame Processing:

   Calls self.process_frame(frame), a method presumably designed to handle specific frame manipulations like motion detection, drawing bounding boxes, and other analytics. This processing could include converting to grayscale, thresholding, contour detection, and updating GUI elements with motion detection data.

4. Error Handling:
   - IndexError: Catches and handles IndexError, which may occur if frame_index is out of the valid range (likely due to asynchronous updates or timing issues in video handling).
   - General Exception: Captures any other exceptions that might be raised during frame fetching or processing. This could be due to issues like corrupted frame data or unexpected interruptions in the video stream.
   - In both error cases, it sets self.paused to True to stop further processing and prevent the application from crashing or behaving unpredictably.

5. GUI Update:

   Regardless of whether the frame was processed successfully or an error occurred, the method updates the frame label by calling self.update_frame_label(). This keeps the displayed frame index in sync with the processing status, which is important for user awareness and application integrity.

Summary

The process_and_display_frame() method encapsulates the logic required to interact with the video data stream, convert frame data formats suitable for processing, handle exceptions gracefully, and ensure consistent updates to the GUI. By managing these tasks within a single method, it centralizes critical video processing operations, enhancing code maintainability and reliability. This method serves as a bridge between raw video data handling and high-level application functionalities, making it a vital part of the video processing workflow in the FrameDifferencer application.

NAVIGATING FRAME

```python
def next_frame(self):
    if self.video and self.frame_index < len(self.video) - 1:  # Check if next frame exists
        self.frame_index += 1
        self.process_and_display_frame()
    else:
        print("No more frames to display.")
        self.paused = True

def prev_frame(self):
    if self.video and self.frame_index > 0:
        self.frame_index -= 1
        self.process_and_display_frame()
    else:
        print("Already at the first frame.")
        self.paused = True
```

The methods next_frame() and prev_frame() in FrameDifferencer class are designed to navigate through the video frames, allowing users to step forward or backward through the video stream manually. These methods are especially useful for detailed analysis and review of specific frames within a video, which is a common requirement in applications involving motion detection and video processing. Let's break down each method's functionality and how they operate:

next_frame() Method
- Purpose: To advance the video to the next frame.
- Operation:
  - Condition Check: First, the method checks if a video is loaded (self.video) and if there is a next frame available (self.frame_index < len(self.video) - 1). The -1 is crucial because frame_index is zero-based, and len(self.video) gives the total number of frames starting from 1.
  - Frame Advancement: If the next frame exists, it increments self.frame_index by 1 to move to the next frame.
  - Frame Processing: Calls self.process_and_display_frame() to handle the fetching, processing, and displaying of the new current frame.
  - End of Video Handling: If there are no more frames to display (i.e., the current frame is the last one), it prints a message indicating this condition and sets self.paused to True to stop any automated playback.

prev_frame() Method
- Purpose: To move the video back to the previous frame.
- Operation:
  - Condition Check: Similar to next_frame, but it checks if the current frame_index is greater than 0, ensuring there's a previous frame to go back to.

- Frame Rewind: If the condition is met, it decrements self.frame_index by 1 to go to the previous frame.
- Frame Processing: Also calls self.process_and_display_frame() to update the GUI with the contents of the now-current frame.
- Start of Video Handling: If already at the first frame (frame_index is 0), it prints a message and sets self.paused to True to prevent further backward movement.

Summary and Use Cases
- User Control: These methods provide essential functionality for user-controlled frame navigation within the video, which is valuable for analyzing events captured in the video in detail. Users can manually step through the video to closely examine changes from frame to frame.
- Error Handling and Feedback: Both methods include feedback mechanisms (print statements) and prevent errors related to frame boundaries (e.g., trying to go past the last frame or before the first frame). This is crucial for maintaining application stability and enhancing user experience by clearly communicating the state of navigation controls.
- Integration with Other Components: By calling self.process_and_display_frame(), these methods integrate closely with the broader functionality of the application, ensuring that any movement between frames is immediately reflected in the application's GUI and that the frame processing logic remains consistent regardless of how the frame index is changed.

These navigation methods make it easier for users to interact with video content directly and meaningfully within the application, an essential feature for any tool designed to handle video analysis tasks such as motion detection, video editing, or forensics analysis.

UPDATING CURRENT FRAME INDEX

```
def update_frame_label(self):
    self.frame_label.config(text=f"Frame: {self.frame_index}")
```

The update_frame_label() method in the FrameDifferencer class serves a simple yet crucial role in the application: it updates the GUI to reflect the current frame index, ensuring that users are always aware of which frame they are viewing or processing. Here's a breakdown of its functionality and significance:

Functionality and Purpose

- Core Function: This method updates the text of a label widget (self.frame_label) on the application's GUI. The label is set to display the current frame index stored in self.frame_index.
- Immediate Feedback: By dynamically updating the label text with text=f"Frame: {self.frame_index}", it provides immediate visual feedback to the user, displaying the index of the current frame being viewed or processed.

Implementation Details

Label Configuration:

- config Method: This is a standard method in Tkinter's Label widget used to modify the widget's options after it has been created. Here, it's used to change the text option, which alters what is displayed on the label.
- Formatted String: The method uses an f-string (f"Frame: {self.frame_index}") to create a string that includes the current value of self.frame_index. This formatting ensures the label accurately reflects the current frame index each time it's updated.

Integration and Use Case
1. When It's Called:

   This method is typically called after the frame index is changed, such as after moving to the next or previous frame, or when a new video is loaded, and the frame index is reset.

2. Role in User Interface:

   It plays an essential role in maintaining synchronization between the actual frame being displayed and the user interface, which helps in enhancing the usability of the application. Users can track their progress through the video and accurately navigate to specific frames based on the index shown.

Importance

- User Orientation: In applications involving video processing or frame-by-frame analysis, it's crucial for users to know the exact position (frame index) they are currently examining. This method facilitates this requirement by ensuring the frame label is always current.

- Error Prevention: By keeping the frame label updated, it prevents user confusion and potential errors in frame navigation or processing. Users are less likely to make mistakes regarding frame-specific operations if they are always informed of their current position in the video stream.

Summary

In summary, the update_frame_label() method, though simple in its functionality, is vital for providing a responsive and informative user experience in the FrameDifferencer application. It ensures that the frame label on the GUI is consistently updated to reflect changes in the frame index, aiding users in their interaction with the application by providing clear and accurate information about the video frames they are viewing. This method exemplifies how fundamental GUI updates are integral to the overall functionality and user-friendliness of interactive applications.

HANDLING MOUSE EVENTS

```python
def on_mousewheel(self, event):
    direction = event.delta // 120
    current_value = int(self.zoom_scale.get())
    if direction == 1 and current_value < 10:
        current_value += 1
    elif direction == -1 and current_value > 1:
        current_value -= 1
    self.zoom_scale.set(current_value)
    self.update_zoom()

def on_press(self, event):
    self.tracker = None
    self.start_x = self.canvas.canvasx(event.x)
    self.start_y = self.canvas.canvasy(event.y)
    # Clear the previous bounding box if it exists
    if self.bbox_rect:
        self.canvas.delete(self.bbox_rect)
        self.bbox_rect = None
    self.bbox = None
    self.bbox2 = None

def on_drag(self, event):
    # Update the endpoint of the rectangle as the mouse moves
    cur_x = self.canvas.canvasx(event.x)
    cur_y = self.canvas.canvasy(event.y)

    # Define the coordinates correctly ensuring x1 < x2 and y1 < y2
    x1, y1 = min(self.start_x, cur_x), min(self.start_y, cur_y)
    x2, y2 = max(self.start_x, cur_x), max(self.start_y, cur_y)

    # Update dimensions for tracking
    self.initial_w = x2 - x1
    self.initial_h = y2 - y1
    self.bbox = (x1, y1, self.initial_w, self.initial_h)
    self.bbox2 = (self.start_x, self.start_y, cur_x, cur_y)

    # Update or create a rectangle on the canvas
    if self.bbox_rect:
```

```
            self.canvas.coords(self.bbox_rect, x1, y1, x2, y2)
        else:
            self.bbox_rect = self.canvas.create_rectangle(x1, y1, x2, y2, 
outline="cyan", width=6)

    def on_release(self, event):
        self.analyze_histogram()   # Call analyze_histogram() method when the mouse 
button is released
```

The methods on_mousewheel(), on_press(), on_drag(), and on_release() are essential for enabling interactive features within your application. Each method provides specific functionalities related to zooming and selection within the GUI's canvas, where video frames are displayed. Let's break down these methods:

on_mousewheel() Method

1. Purpose: Handles zooming in and out based on the mouse wheel movement.
2. Implementation:
   - Direction Calculation: The direction and intensity of the mouse wheel scroll are determined using event.delta. The value is normalized by dividing by 120 (a common factor for mouse wheel events).
   - Zoom Adjustment: Depending on the scroll direction, it increments or decrements the current_value of zoom_scale, a scale widget presumably used to represent zoom level.
   - Boundary Conditions: It ensures that the zoom level remains within a defined range (between 1 and 10).
   - Update Zoom: Calls self.update_zoom() to apply the new zoom level to the displayed frame.

on_press() Method

1. Purpose: Initiates a selection or tracking process when the mouse button is pressed.
2. Implementation:

- Starting Point: Captures the initial coordinates (start_x, start_y) where the mouse button was pressed.
- Reset: Clears any existing bounding box (bbox_rect) to prepare for a new selection. This is important for functionalities like selecting a region for detailed analysis or tracking.

on_drag() Method

1. Purpose: Updates the bounding box dynamically as the user drags the mouse, allowing real-time visual feedback of the selected area.
2. Implementation:
    - Dynamic Coordinates: Continuously updates the coordinates (x1, y1, x2, y2) to adjust the bounding box as the mouse moves.
    - Rectangle Drawing: If a rectangle (bbox_rect) exists, it updates its coordinates; if not, it creates a new rectangle on the canvas. This visual representation helps users precisely define the area they are interested in.

on_release() Method

1. Purpose: Finalizes the selection when the mouse button is released and potentially triggers further analysis based on the selected region.
2. Implementation:
Analyze Histogram: Calls self.analyze_histogram(), which presumably analyzes the selected region's pixel data, such as calculating color histograms or other statistical data.

Summary

- User Interaction: These methods together provide an interactive mechanism for users to zoom in/out and select areas of interest within video frames. Such features are particularly useful in applications involving image analysis, where users need to focus on specific parts of an image or track motion manually.

- Functional Cohesion: Each method contributes to a seamless interactive experience by handling different aspects of mouse interactions, making the GUI more intuitive and responsive.
- Enhanced Analysis Capability: The ability to select areas and analyze them further (as hinted by analyze_histogram) allows for detailed examination of video data, which is essential for tasks such as object detection, motion analysis, or even educational purposes to study image characteristics.

By implementing these methods, you enhance the overall functionality and user-friendliness of your application, enabling users to interact effectively with complex video data through simple mouse actions.

ANALYZING HISTOGRAM

```python
def analyze_histogram(self):
    if self.bbox2 is not None and self.video:
        x1, y1, x2, y2 = map(int, self.bbox2)
        if x1 != x2 and y1 != y2:
            try:
                frame = self.video.get_data(self.frame_index)
                # Ensure the bounding box is within the frame boundaries
                h, w, _ = frame.shape
                x1, x2 = max(0, min(x1, w)), max(0, min(x2, w))
                y1, y2 = max(0, min(y1, h)), max(0, min(y2, h))

                # Ensure x1 < x2 and y1 < y2
                x1, x2 = sorted([x1, x2])
                y1, y2 = sorted([y1, y2])

                cropped_frame = frame[y1:y2, x1:x2]
                if cropped_frame.size > 0:
                    cropped_frame = cv2.cvtColor(cropped_frame, cv2.COLOR_BGR2RGB)
```

```
                    # Get selected filter from combobox
                    selected_filter = self.filter_combobox.get()
                    # Apply selected filter
                    filtered_frame = self.apply_filter(selected_filter, cropped_frame)

                    self.create_popup_window(filtered_frame)
                    self.display_cropped_image(filtered_frame)
                    self.display_histograms(filtered_frame)
                else:
                    print("Cropped frame is empty.")
            except Exception as e:
                print("Failed to process frame:", e)
        else:
            print("Bounding box dimensions are zero or negative.")
```

The analyze_histogram() method in FrameDifferencer class is a sophisticated function designed to analyze a specific region of a video frame, based on user selection. This method is essential for tasks that require detailed analysis of pixel data within a bounded area, such as color analysis, filter effects, or statistical studies on video content. Here's a detailed breakdown of the method's operations and functionalities:

Method Overview

- Purpose: To analyze the selected region of a video frame for histograms and apply selected filters to the region, which is then displayed in a popup window.
- Use Case: Useful in applications like video editing, scientific imaging, or security where detailed inspection of a frame region is required.

Step-by-Step Execution

1. Bounding Box Validation:
    - Existence Check: Confirms that a bounding box (bbox2) has been defined and that a video is loaded.
    - Dimension Check: Ensures that the bounding box has non-zero dimensions, indicating that an actual area has been selected.

2. Frame Retrieval and Boundary Adjustment:
    - Retrieve Frame: Fetches the current frame based on self.frame_index.
    - Boundary Safety: Adjusts the coordinates of the bounding box to ensure they are within the frame's dimensions, preventing out-of-bound errors when accessing the frame data.
    - Coordinate Sorting: Ensures the coordinates are correctly ordered (x1 < x2 and y1 < y2), crucial for accurately defining the rectangle slice.
3. Region Cropping and Filtering:
    - Crop Frame: Slices the frame to get the specified region. This cropped frame is then used for further analysis.
    - Color Space Conversion: Converts the cropped region from BGR to RGB to match the expected color space for display and analysis.
4. Filter Application:
    - Retrieves the user-selected filter from a combobox.
    - Applies this filter using self.apply_filter, which modifies the cropped frame based on the chosen filter's effect.
5. Display and Analysis:
    - Popup Window Creation: Creates a new popup window to display the results.
    - Display Cropped Image: Shows the filtered cropped image in the popup window.
    - Display Histograms: Generates and displays histograms for the cropped area, providing insights into the color distribution and intensity levels within the selected region.

Error Handling
- Empty Region Check: Checks if the cropped region has any pixel data. If not, it outputs a message indicating that the selected area is empty.

- Exception Handling: Catches and logs any exceptions that occur during the process, which could be due to issues with frame data retrieval, cropping, or filtering.

Integration and User Interaction
- Integration with GUI Components: The method is closely integrated with GUI components like the combobox for filter selection, enhancing the interactive nature of the application.
- User Feedback: Provides feedback through console messages about the status of the operation, such as errors or empty selections, which helps users understand the application's state and respond accordingly.

Summary

The analyze_histogram() method effectively combines image processing, GUI interaction, and error handling to provide a robust tool for analyzing specific regions within video frames. This functionality is vital for detailed pixel-level analysis and enhances the application's utility in fields requiring precise image examination. By allowing users to select, filter, and analyze regions interactively, it significantly boosts the analytical capabilities of the Frame Differencer application.

CREATINNG POPUP WINDOW

```
def create_popup_window(self, cropped_frame):
    self.popup_window = tk.Toplevel(self.master)
    self.popup_window.title("Cropped Image and Its Histogram")
    self.popup_window.geometry("1500x700")

def display_cropped_image(self, cropped_frame):
    cropped_frame_frame = tk.Frame(self.popup_window)
```

```
    cropped_frame_frame.pack(side="left")

    cropped_frame_rgb = cv2.cvtColor(cropped_frame, cv2.COLOR_BGR2RGB)
    cropped_img = Image.fromarray(cropped_frame_rgb)
    cropped_img = cropped_img.resize((600, 600))

    cropped_photo = ImageTk.PhotoImage(cropped_img)
    cropped_canvas = tk.Canvas(cropped_frame_frame, width=600, height=600)
    cropped_canvas.pack(side="left", anchor="nw")
    cropped_canvas.create_image(0, 0, anchor="nw", image=cropped_photo)
    cropped_canvas.image = cropped_photo
```

The methods create_popup_window() and display_cropped_image() are designed to enhance user interaction by visually presenting the results of specific image analyses performed within your application. These methods demonstrate the integration of image processing results with GUI elements to provide a rich user experience. Let's delve into each method's functionality:

create_popup_window() Method

1. Purpose: This method initializes a new top-level window that serves as a popup to display the cropped image and its associated histograms.
2. Functionality:
    3. Toplevel Creation: Uses tk.Toplevel(self.master) to create a new window that is a child of the main application window (master). This window will pop up in front of the main application window but remains part of the same application.
    4. Window Title: Sets the title of the window to "Cropped Image and Its Histogram" to clearly indicate the content and purpose of the window.
    5. Window Size: Defines the size of the popup window as "1500x700" pixels. This dimension is chosen to provide ample space for displaying both the cropped image and the histograms side by side.

display_cropped_image() Method

1. Purpose: To display the cropped image in the previously created popup window, ensuring that the image is clearly visible and well-presented.
2. Functionality:
   - Frame Setup: A tk.Frame is created and packed to the left side of the popup window. This frame acts as a container for the image canvas.
   - Color Conversion: Converts the cropped image from BGR to RGB. This conversion is necessary because OpenCV handles images in BGR format by default, whereas graphical display systems including Tkinter's ImageTk.PhotoImage expect RGB format.
   - Image Resizing: Resizes the image to 600x600 pixels using Pillow. This step ensures that the image fits well within the display area without losing significant detail.
   - PhotoImage Creation: Converts the Pillow image object to a ImageTk.PhotoImage, which can be displayed on a Tkinter canvas.
   - Canvas Setup: A tk.Canvas is packed into the frame with the specified width and height of 600x600 pixels. This canvas serves as the display surface for the image.
   - Image Display: Places the image on the canvas at the top-left corner (anchor="nw"). This method ensures that the image is displayed correctly and keeps a reference to the PhotoImage object in cropped_canvas.image to prevent it from being garbage-collected.

Integration and User Experience

- Integration: These methods work closely together to enhance the visual presentation of results within your application. By separating the creation of the popup window and the display of the image into two methods, you maintain a clean and modular code structure.

- User Interaction: The popup window provides an interactive and user-friendly way to view detailed results of specific operations, such as the analysis performed on selected regions of a video frame. It allows users to visually inspect the effects of different filters and understand the pixel distribution through histograms.

Summary

These methods, create_popup_window() and display_cropped_image(), exemplify good practices in GUI programming by encapsulating functionality into specific, focused methods, and enhancing user interaction by providing clear and detailed visualizations of processing results. They demonstrate the effective use of Tkinter's capabilities for creating and managing GUI components dynamically based on application processing outputs.

DISPLAYING HISTOGRAM OF CROPPED IMAGE

```python
def display_histograms(self, cropped_frame):
    histograms_frame = tk.Frame(self.popup_window)
    histograms_frame.pack(side="right", padx=20)

    self.display_line_histogram(cropped_frame, histograms_frame)
    self.display_bar_histogram(cropped_frame, histograms_frame)

def display_line_histogram(self, cropped_frame, histograms_frame):
    line_histogram_frame = tk.Frame(histograms_frame)
    line_histogram_frame.pack(side="top", pady=10)

    plt.figure(figsize=(12, 4))
    color = ('r', 'g', 'b')
    for i, col in enumerate(color):
        histr = cv2.calcHist([cropped_frame], [i], None, [256], [0, 256])
        plt.plot(histr, color=col, label=f'Channel {col.upper()}', linewidth=2)
        plt.xlim([0, 256])
    plt.title('Line Histogram')
```

```python
        plt.xlabel('Pixel Value')
        plt.ylabel('Frequency')
        plt.tight_layout()
        plt.grid(True)
        plt.legend()

        line_histogram_img = self.plot_to_image(plt)
        self.display_histogram_image(line_histogram_frame, line_histogram_img)

    def display_bar_histogram(self, cropped_frame, histograms_frame):
        bar_histogram_frame = tk.Frame(histograms_frame)
        bar_histogram_frame.pack(side="bottom", pady=10)

        plt.figure(figsize=(12, 4))
        color = ('r', 'g', 'b')
        for i, col in enumerate(color):
            hist_range = (0, 256)
            hist_counts, _ = np.histogram(cropped_frame[:, :, i], bins=64, range=hist_range)
            plt.bar(np.arange(64), hist_counts, color=col, alpha=0.7, label=f'Channel {col.upper()}')
            for index, value in enumerate(hist_counts):
                plt.text(index, value + 10, str(int(value)), ha='center', va='bottom', fontsize=9)

        plt.title('Bar Histogram')
        plt.xlabel('Pixel Value')
        plt.ylabel('Frequency')
        plt.xticks(np.linspace(0, 63, num=5), np.linspace(0, 255, num=5, dtype=int))
        # Adjust x-axis ticks
        plt.tight_layout()
        plt.grid(True)
        plt.legend()

        bar_histogram_img = self.plot_to_image(plt)
        self.display_histogram_image(bar_histogram_frame, bar_histogram_img)

    def display_histogram_image(self, parent_frame, img):
        histogram_photo = ImageTk.PhotoImage(image=img)
        histogram_canvas = tk.Canvas(parent_frame, width=900, height=300)
        histogram_canvas.pack(side="bottom", anchor="se")
        histogram_canvas.create_image(0, 0, anchor="nw", image=histogram_photo)
        histogram_canvas.image = histogram_photo

    def plot_histogram_bar_to_image(self, image):
        # Calculate histogram for each channel
        histograms = []
        for i in range(3):
```

```python
            hist_range = (0, 256)
            hist_counts, _ = np.histogram(image[:, :, i], bins=64, range=hist_range)
# Adjust bins to 64
            histograms.append(hist_counts)

        # Extracting only 64 bins from the histogram
        num_bins = 64  # Adjusted to 64 bins

        # Generating colors for each channel
        colors = ['red', 'green', 'blue']

        plt.figure()
        for i, histogram in enumerate(histograms):
            # Normalize the histogram counts for better visualization
            hist_counts = histogram / np.sum(histogram)
            # Setting the color for each channel
            plt.bar(np.arange(num_bins), hist_counts[:num_bins], color=colors[i],
alpha=0.7, label=f'Channel {["Red", "Green", "Blue"][i]}')

        plt.xlabel('Pixel Value')
        plt.ylabel('Normalized Frequency')
        plt.title('RGB Channel Histograms')
        plt.grid(True)
        plt.tight_layout()
        plt.legend()

        # Convert the histogram bar graph to an image
        histogram_bar_img = self.plot_to_image(plt)
        histogram_bar_photo = ImageTk.PhotoImage(image=histogram_bar_img)

        return histogram_bar_photo

    def plot_to_image(self, plt):
        plt.savefig('temp_plot.png')
        img = Image.open('temp_plot.png')
        return img
```

The methods here (display_histograms(), display_line_histogram(), display_bar_histogram(), display_histogram_image(), and plot_to_image()) are designed to create and display histograms for a cropped image region within a popup window. These histograms are valuable for analyzing the pixel intensity distribution across different color channels. Let's review these methods and how they function together:

display_histograms() Method

1. Purpose: To set up the environment for displaying both line and bar histograms of the cropped image.
2. Implementation:
   - Histogram Frame Setup: A tk.Frame is created within the popup window and packed to the right side. This frame serves as the container for both line and bar histogram displays.
   - Display Functions Call: Calls display_line_histogram() and display_bar_histogram() to generate and display each histogram type.

display_line_histogram() Method

1. Purpose: To generate and display a line histogram for the RGB channels of the cropped image.
2. Implementation:
   - Line Histogram Frame: Establishes a sub-frame for the line histogram display.
   - Histogram Calculation: Uses OpenCV's calcHist function to calculate histograms for each color channel.
   - Plotting: Utilizes Matplotlib to plot these histograms with different colors for each channel and annotates the graph with axes labels and a legend.
   - Conversion to Display: Converts the plotted histogram to a format suitable for Tkinter display using the plot_to_image method() and then displays it using display_histogram_image().

display_bar_histogram() Method

1. Purpose: To generate and display a bar histogram for the RGB channels of the cropped image.

2. Implementation:
   - Bar Histogram Frame: Sets up another sub-frame specifically for the bar histogram.
   - Histogram Calculation: Uses NumPy's histogram function to compute the histogram for each channel.
   - Plotting: Uses Matplotlib to plot bar graphs, enhancing visualization with color differentiation, text annotations on bars, and customized x-axis ticks.
   - Conversion and Display: Converts the plot to an image and displays it in the GUI, similar to the line histogram method.

display_histogram_image() Method
1. Purpose: To display a histogram image on a Tkinter canvas within the provided frame.
2. Implementation:
   - Canvas Setup: Creates a canvas in the specified frame, sized appropriately for the histogram image.
   - Image Display: Places the image on the canvas, ensuring it is retained in memory by storing it as an attribute of the canvas.

plot_to_image() Method
1. Purpose: To convert a Matplotlib plot into an image format that can be displayed in Tkinter.
2. Implementation:
   - File Saving: Saves the plot to a temporary PNG file.
   - Image Conversion: Opens the saved file using PIL and returns the image object.

Summary and Utility

These methods collectively provide comprehensive histogram analysis and visualization capabilities within your application, crucial for detailed pixel-level analysis in image processing tasks. By combining OpenCV for data manipulation, Matplotlib for creating visual representations, and Tkinter for GUI displays, these methods effectively bridge the gap between data processing and user interaction.

This integrated approach allows users to visually interpret the color intensity distributions of selected image regions, which can be instrumental in applications ranging from photo editing to scientific research where such data is critical.

HANDLING IMAGE FILTERING

```python
def apply_filter(self, filter_name, frame):
    if filter_name == "None":
        return frame
    elif filter_name == "Gaussian":
        return cv2.GaussianBlur(frame, (5, 5), 0)
    elif filter_name == "Mean":
        return cv2.blur(frame, (5, 5))
    elif filter_name == "Median":
        return cv2.medianBlur(frame, 5)
    elif filter_name == "Bilateral Filtering":
        return cv2.bilateralFilter(frame, 9, 75, 75)
    elif filter_name == "Non-local Means Denoising":
        return cv2.fastNlMeansDenoisingColored(frame, None, 10, 10, 7, 21)
    elif filter_name == "Anisotropic Diffusion":
        return self.anisotropic_diffusion(frame)
    elif filter_name == "Total Variation Denoising":
        return self.total_variation_denoising(frame)
    elif filter_name == "Wiener Filter":
        return self.wiener_filter(frame)
    elif filter_name == "Adaptive Thresholding":
        return self.adaptive_threshold_each_channel(frame)
    elif filter_name == "Haar Wavelet Transform":
        return self.haar_wavelet_transform(frame)
    elif filter_name == "Daubechies Wavelet Transform":
```

```
        return self.daubechies_wavelet_transform(frame)
else:
        return frame  # Default: return original frame if filter not found
```

The apply_filter() method in FrameDifferencer class is designed to handle a range of different image processing filters, enabling users to apply various effects to frames based on their selection. Each filter type has specific attributes and applications that can significantly alter the image data for various purposes, such as noise reduction, detail enhancement, or data extraction. Here's an overview of each filter and its typical use case within the context of the method:

Overview of Filters

1. None:
    - Effect: Returns the frame as is without any modifications.
    - Use Case: Useful when users want to analyze the original frame without any processing.
2. Gaussian Blur:
    - Effect: Applies a Gaussian blur with a kernel size of (5, 5).
    - Use Case: Reduces image noise and detail by smoothing the frame, which is helpful for reducing high-frequency noise.
3. Mean (Averaging) Blur:
    - Effect: Blurs an image using the normalized box filter.
    - Use Case: Similar to Gaussian blur, it smooths the image but uses a simple arithmetic mean of pixels within the kernel window.
4. Median Blur:
    - Effect: Applies a median blur with a kernel size of 5.
    - Use Case: Effective in removing salt-and-pepper noise from images while preserving edges better than Gaussian or mean blurs.
5. Bilateral Filtering:

- Effect: Applies bilateral filtering which can reduce unwanted noise while keeping edges sharp.
- Use Case: Useful for detailed edge-preserving smoothing, often used in applications where edge integrity is crucial.

6. Non-local Means Denoising:
   - Effect: Uses the Non-local Means Denoising algorithm to remove noise while preserving details.
   - Use Case: Ideal for reducing noise in photos or video frames where detail preservation is critical.

7. Anisotropic Diffusion:
   - Effect: Calls a custom method (not detailed here) which presumably implements anisotropic diffusion (also known as Perona-Malik filter).
   - Use Case: Helps in noise reduction and edge enhancement based on the image's local content.

8. Total Variation Denoising:
   - Effect: Another custom method likely involving denoising that aims to reduce total variation in the image, smoothing out textures while preserving edges and contours.
   - Use Case: Used in applications where a piecewise smooth representation of image content is desirable.

9. Wiener Filter:
   - Effect: A conceptual implementation of the Wiener filter which might include using the cv2.medianBlur and cv2.fastNlMeansDenoising as placeholders for actual Wiener filter operations.
   - Use Case: Traditionally used to reduce noise from the image presumed to be additive Gaussian noise.

10. Adaptive Thresholding:

- Effect: Applies adaptive thresholding to each channel separately, which can help in segmenting foreground from background dynamically.
- Use Case: Useful in scenarios where lighting conditions vary across different parts of the image.

11. Haar Wavelet Transform:
    - Effect: Performs a Haar wavelet transform to decompose the image into different frequency components.
    - Use Case: Can be used for image compression, feature extraction, or denoising.

12. Daubechies Wavelet Transform:
    - Effect: Applies a Daubechies wavelet transform, which is similar to the Haar transform but with smoother wavelets and better energy compaction properties.
    - Use Case: Useful in advanced image processing tasks such as denoising, compression, or even in financial signal analysis.

Method Implementation

Each branch of the if-elif chain checks the filter name provided and applies the corresponding image processing operation. This approach allows users to dynamically change the processing behavior of the application based on their needs, providing flexibility in image analysis. By offering a variety of filters, the application can cater to diverse requirements, from simple visualization improvements to complex analysis tasks. This functionality enhances the utility of the application in educational, experimental, or professional settings where image processing is a key component.

DEFINING FILTERS

```python
    def wiener_filter(self, frame, kernel_size=(5, 5), noise_var=0.01):
        # Check if frame is None
        if frame is None:
            print("Error: Input frame is None.")
            return None

        # Check if frame is a valid numpy array
        if not isinstance(frame, np.ndarray):
            print("Error: Input frame is not a numpy array.")
            return None

        # Check if frame is an empty array
        if frame.size == 0:
            print("Error: Input frame is empty.")
            return None

        # Check if frame is in BGR color space
        if frame.shape[-1] != 3:
            print("Error: Input frame is not in BGR color space.")
            return None

        # Apply Wiener filter
        filtered_frame = cv2.medianBlur(frame, kernel_size[0])  # Use kernel_size[0] as the kernel size
        filtered_frame = cv2.fastNlMeansDenoising(filtered_frame, h=noise_var)
        return filtered_frame

    def adaptive_threshold_each_channel(self, frame):
        # Split the frame into individual channels
        b, g, r = cv2.split(frame)

        # Apply adaptive thresholding to each channel separately
        b_thresh = cv2.adaptiveThreshold(b, 255, cv2.ADAPTIVE_THRESH_GAUSSIAN_C, cv2.THRESH_BINARY, 11, 2)
        g_thresh = cv2.adaptiveThreshold(g, 255, cv2.ADAPTIVE_THRESH_GAUSSIAN_C, cv2.THRESH_BINARY, 11, 2)
        r_thresh = cv2.adaptiveThreshold(r, 255, cv2.ADAPTIVE_THRESH_GAUSSIAN_C, cv2.THRESH_BINARY, 11, 2)

        # Merge the thresholded channels back together
        return cv2.merge([b_thresh, g_thresh, r_thresh])

    def haar_wavelet_transform(self, frame):
        # Split the frame into its individual color channels
```

```python
        b, g, r = cv2.split(frame)

        # Perform the wavelet transform on each channel separately
        b_coeffs = pywt.dwt2(b, 'haar')
        g_coeffs = pywt.dwt2(g, 'haar')
        r_coeffs = pywt.dwt2(r, 'haar')

        # Reconstruct the channels from the coefficients
        b_reconstructed = pywt.idwt2(b_coeffs, 'haar')
        g_reconstructed = pywt.idwt2(g_coeffs, 'haar')
        r_reconstructed = pywt.idwt2(r_coeffs, 'haar')

        # Clip the values to ensure they are within the valid range
        b_reconstructed = np.clip(b_reconstructed, 0, 255).astype(np.uint8)
        g_reconstructed = np.clip(g_reconstructed, 0, 255).astype(np.uint8)
        r_reconstructed = np.clip(r_reconstructed, 0, 255).astype(np.uint8)

        # Merge the channels back together
        return cv2.merge([b_reconstructed, g_reconstructed, r_reconstructed])

    def daubechies_wavelet_transform(self, frame):
        # Split the frame into its individual color channels
        b, g, r = cv2.split(frame)

        # Choose the wavelet function (Daubechies 5)
        wavelet = 'db5'

        # Perform the wavelet transform on each channel separately
        b_coeffs = pywt.dwt2(b, wavelet)
        g_coeffs = pywt.dwt2(g, wavelet)
        r_coeffs = pywt.dwt2(r, wavelet)

        # Reconstruct the channels from the coefficients
        b_reconstructed = pywt.idwt2(b_coeffs, wavelet)
        g_reconstructed = pywt.idwt2(g_coeffs, wavelet)
        r_reconstructed = pywt.idwt2(r_coeffs, wavelet)

        # Clip the values to ensure they are within the valid range
        b_reconstructed = np.clip(b_reconstructed, 0, 255).astype(np.uint8)
        g_reconstructed = np.clip(g_reconstructed, 0, 255).astype(np.uint8)
        r_reconstructed = np.clip(r_reconstructed, 0, 255).astype(np.uint8)

        # Merge the channels back together
        return cv2.merge([b_reconstructed, g_reconstructed, r_reconstructed])

    def anisotropic_diffusion(self, img):
        return cv2.fastNlMeansDenoisingColored(img, None, 10, 10, 7, 21)
```

```python
    def apply_total_variation_denoising_channel(self, channel, weight, iterations):
        # Initialize the result with the original channel
        result = channel.copy().astype(np.float64)  # Convert to float64

        # Perform total variation denoising
        for _ in range(iterations):
            # Compute the gradient of the channel
            dx = cv2.Sobel(result, cv2.CV_64F, 1, 0, ksize=3)
            dy = cv2.Sobel(result, cv2.CV_64F, 0, 1, ksize=3)

            # Update the channel using the gradient and the weight
            result -= weight * np.sqrt(dx**2 + dy**2)

        # Clip the values to ensure they are within the valid range
        result = np.clip(result, 0, 255).astype(np.uint8)

        return result

    def total_variation_denoising(self, img, weight=0.01, iterations=20):
        # Split the image into its individual color channels
        b, g, r = cv2.split(img)

        # Apply total variation denoising to each channel separately
        b_denoised = self.apply_total_variation_denoising_channel(b, weight, iterations)
        g_denoised = self.apply_total_variation_denoising_channel(g, weight, iterations)
        r_denoised = self.apply_total_variation_denoising_channel(r, weight, iterations)

        # Merge the denoised channels back together
        return cv2.merge([b_denoised, g_denoised, r_denoised])
```

Wiener Filter Method

This method approximates a Wiener filter using median blurring and non-local means denoising to reduce noise in images.

Steps:

1. Input Validation: First, it checks if the input frame is None, not a numpy array, empty, or not in BGR color space, handling each case with an appropriate error message.

2. Median Blurring: Applies a median blur with the specified kernel size to reduce noise. Median blurring is effective at removing salt-and-pepper noise while preserving edges.
3. Non-local Means Denoising: Further processes the blurred image using non-local means denoising, which compares all patches in the image and averages similar ones to reduce noise while preserving details.
4. Output: Returns the denoised image.

Adaptive Thresholding Method

This method applies adaptive thresholding independently to each color channel of an image.

Steps:

1. Channel Splitting: Splits the BGR image into its individual blue, green, and red channels.
2. Adaptive Threshold Application: Applies an adaptive threshold to each channel. This method calculates thresholds for small regions, allowing for variable lighting.
3. Channel Merging: Re-combines the thresholded channels back into a single BGR image.
4. Output: Returns the color image where each channel has been thresholded independently.

Haar Wavelet Transform Method

Performs a discrete wavelet transform using Haar wavelets, useful for image compression and noise reduction.

Steps:

1. Channel Splitting: Separates the image into its three primary color channels.

2. Wavelet Transformation: Applies the Haar wavelet transform to each channel individually.
3. Inverse Wavelet Transformation: Applies the inverse transform to reconstruct the image from the wavelet coefficients.
4. Clipping and Type Conversion: Ensures that pixel values are within the valid range (0-255) and converts them back to 8-bit integers.
5. Channel Merging: Merges the processed channels back into a single image.
6. Output: Returns the reconstructed image.

Daubechies Wavelet Transform Method

Uses Daubechies wavelets for a more sophisticated wavelet transform, which is particularly good at capturing higher frequency details.

Steps:
1. Channel Splitting: Like the Haar method, it begins by splitting the image into its color components.
2. Wavelet Transformation: Applies the Daubechies wavelet transform separately to each channel.
3. Inverse Transformation: Each channel is reconstructed from its wavelet coefficients.
4. Clipping and Conversion: Ensures pixel values are properly bounded and of the correct data type.
5. Channel Merging: Combines the channels back into a single BGR image.
6. Output: Outputs the fully processed image.

Anisotropic Diffusion Method

Simulates anisotropic diffusion for edge-preserving smoothing.

Steps:

1. Non-local Means Denoising: Directly uses OpenCV's function to denoise the image while attempting to preserve edges, approximating anisotropic diffusion's effect.
2. Output: Returns the denoised image.

Total Variation Denoising Method

Reduces the total variation in the image, maintaining important edges.

Steps:
1. Channel Splitting: The image is split into red, green, and blue components.
2. Denoising Each Channel: Each channel is denoised using a custom method that applies total variation denoising. This involves calculating the gradient of the channel, adjusting the pixel values based on the gradient, and repeating this for a set number of iterations.
3. Channel Merging: The denoised channels are merged back together.
4. Output: The method returns the color image with reduced noise.

Each of these methods demonstrates advanced techniques in image processing that can be applied to various fields such as digital photography, video processing, and scientific visualization. By understanding the steps involved in each method, you can better utilize and adapt these techniques for specific applications.

ENTRY POINT FOR APPLICATION

```
def main():
    root = tk.Tk()
    app = FrameDifferencer(root)
    root.mainloop()
```

```
if __name__ == "__main__":
    main()
```

The code is the entry point for a Tkinter-based graphical user interface (GUI) application. It sets up and runs an application that likely involves frame differencing, as indicated by the use of a class named FrameDifferencer. Here's a breakdown of each part of the code and what it does:

Code Explanation

1. main Function:
   - root = tk.Tk(): This line creates the main window for the Tkinter application. Tk() is a class in Tkinter used to create a top-level widget of Tk which usually serves as the main window of an application.
   - app = FrameDifferencer(root): Here, an instance of the FrameDifferencer class is created. The root window, which is the main window of the application, is passed to it. This suggests that FrameDifferencer is designed to act as the main interface for the application, handling all the GUI components and their interactions. The FrameDifferencer class is expected to be defined elsewhere in your code, where it sets up the layout, widgets, and functionalities specific to what the application is meant to do, likely involving processing video frames for motion detection.
   - root.mainloop(): This line starts the Tkinter event loop. The event loop is necessary for processing user actions such as button clicks, mouse movements, keyboard presses, or other interactions. The mainloop() function is a blocking call that waits for events from the user and processes them until the application window is closed.
2. Entry Point Check:
   - if __name__ == "__main__":: This conditional statement checks whether the module is being run as the main program. This check is standard in Python scripts to ensure that the code block runs only if the script is executed directly (not when

imported as a module in another script). This is where the main() function gets called if the condition is true.

RUNNING PROGRAM

Run program and click on Play/Pause button. Or, you can choose certain frame by pushing Next Frame button. Then, draw a bounding box rectangle on certain object in the frame and push Next Frame button.

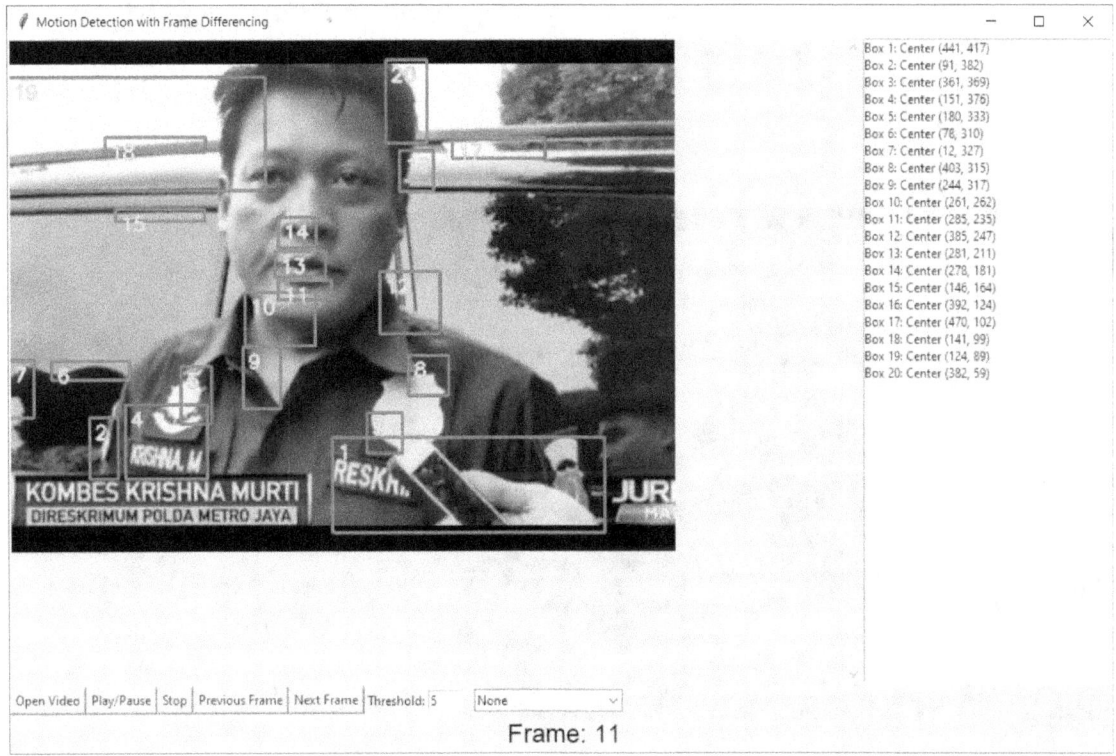

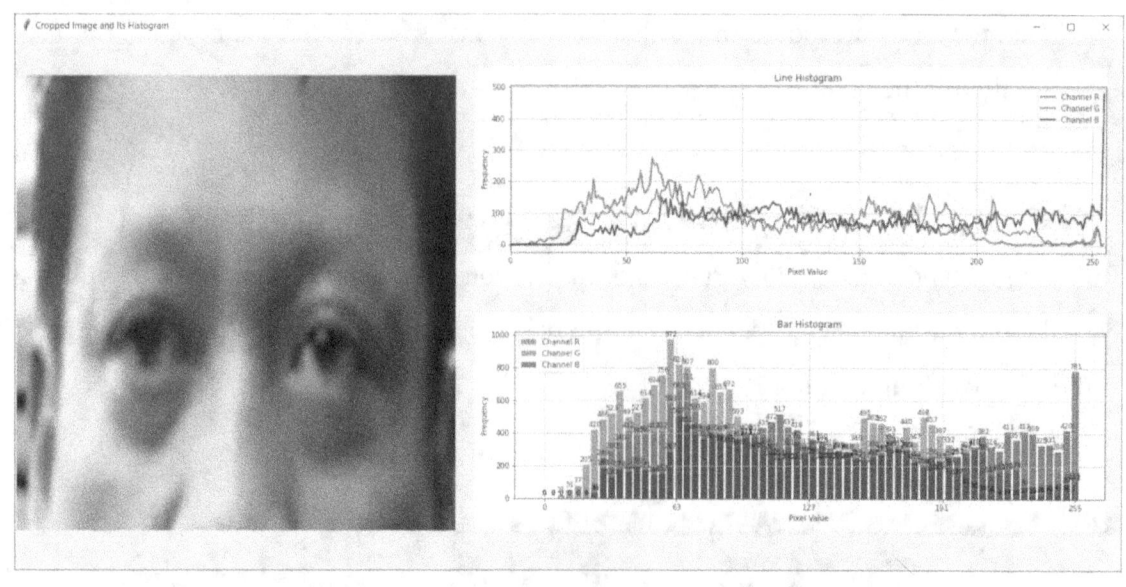

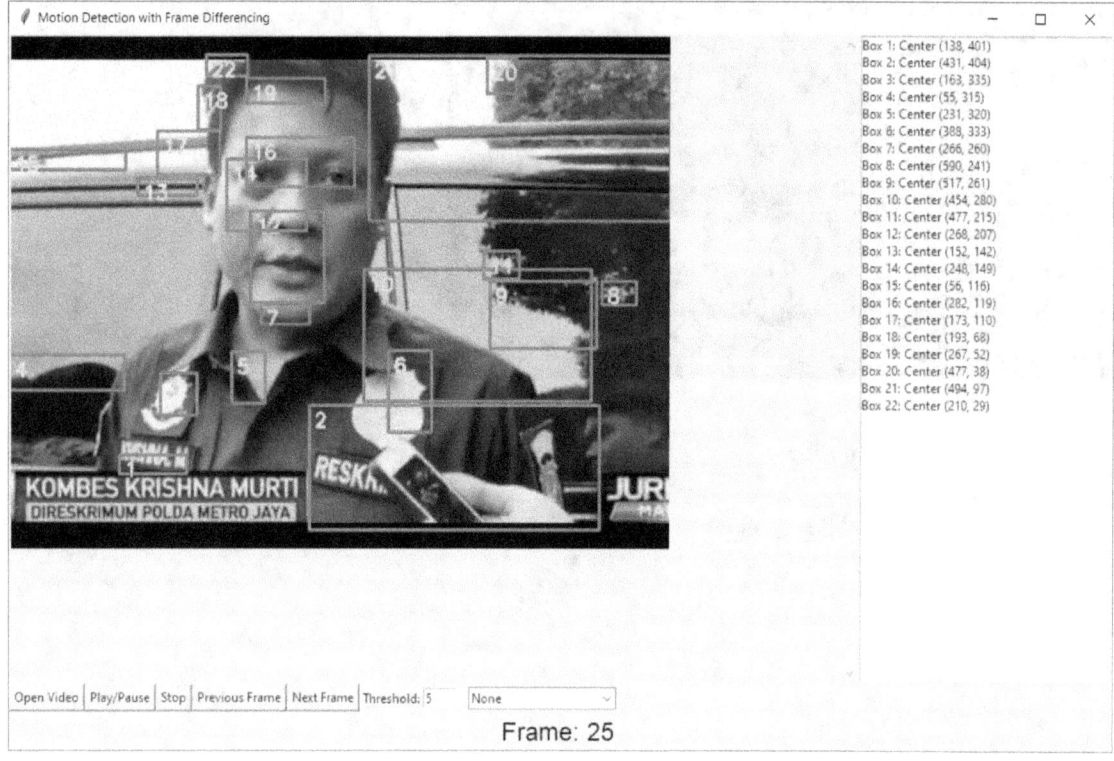

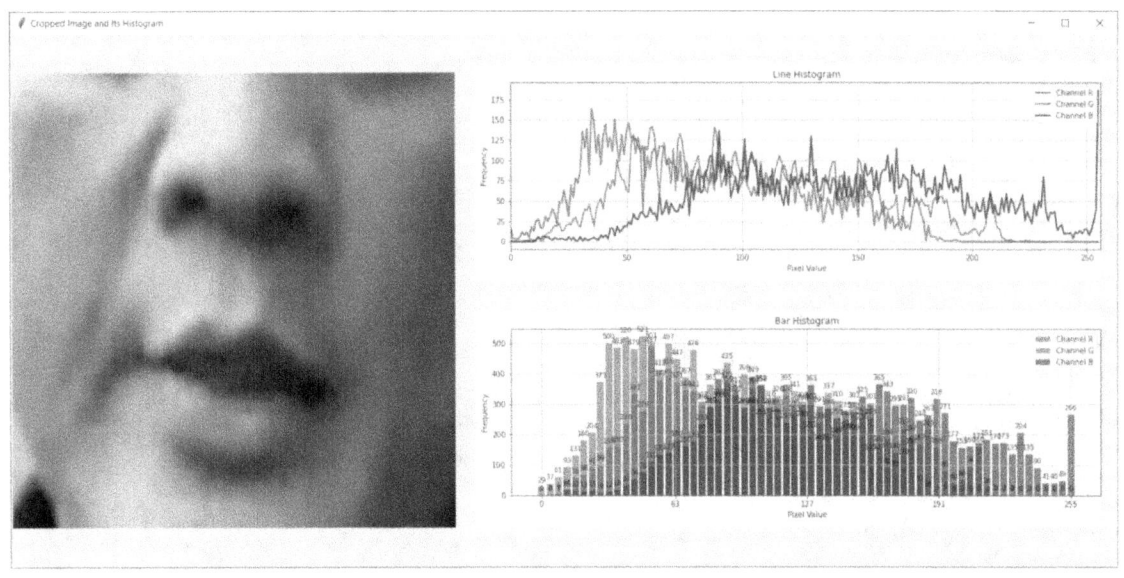

SOURCE CODE

```
#frame_differencing.py
import tkinter as tk
from tkinter import ttk
from tkinter import filedialog
from PIL import Image, ImageTk
import cv2
import imageio
import matplotlib.pyplot as plt
import pywt
import numpy as np

class FrameDifferencer:
    def __init__(self, master):
        self.master = master
        self.master.title("Motion Detection with Frame Differencing")
        self.bbox_rect = None  # Initialize bbox_rect attribute to None

        # Video related variables
        self.video = None
        self.previous_frame = None
        self.frame_index = 0
        self.paused = True
        self.threshold = 5  # Default threshold for frame differencing
```

```python
        # Creates widgets
        self.create_widgets(master)

    def create_widgets(self, master):
        # Create a frame for the canvas and listbox
        display_frame = tk.Frame(master)
        display_frame.pack(fill=tk.BOTH, expand=True)

        # Set up the canvas
        self.canvas = tk.Canvas(display_frame, width=800, height=600)
        self.canvas.pack(side=tk.LEFT, fill=tk.BOTH, expand=True)
        self.canvas.bind("<MouseWheel>", self.on_mousewheel)
        self.canvas.bind("<ButtonPress-1>", self.on_press)
        self.canvas.bind("<B1-Motion>", self.on_drag)
        self.canvas.bind("<ButtonRelease-1>", self.on_release)  # Bind ButtonRelease event

        # Set up the listbox for displaying centers
        self.listbox = tk.Listbox(display_frame, width=40, height=20)
        self.listbox.pack(side=tk.RIGHT, fill=tk.Y)

        # Add scrollbar to the listbox
        scrollbar = tk.Scrollbar(display_frame, orient="vertical", command=self.listbox.yview)
        scrollbar.pack(side=tk.RIGHT, fill=tk.Y)
        self.listbox.config(yscrollcommand=scrollbar.set)

        # Control Panel below the display frame
        control_panel = tk.Frame(master)
        control_panel.pack(fill=tk.X)

        self.open_button = tk.Button(control_panel, text="Open Video", command=self.open_video)
        self.open_button.pack(side=tk.LEFT)

        self.play_button = tk.Button(control_panel, text="Play/Pause", command=self.toggle_play_pause)
        self.play_button.pack(side=tk.LEFT)

        self.stop_button = tk.Button(control_panel, text="Stop", command=self.stop_video)
        self.stop_button.pack(side=tk.LEFT)

        self.prev_button = tk.Button(control_panel, text="Previous Frame", command=self.prev_frame)
        self.prev_button.pack(side=tk.LEFT)
```

```python
        self.next_button = tk.Button(control_panel, text="Next Frame",
command=self.next_frame)
        self.next_button.pack(side=tk.LEFT)

        # Frame number label
        self.frame_label = tk.Label(master, text="Frame: 0", font=('Helvetica', 18))
        self.frame_label.pack()

        # Threshold Control
        self.threshold_label = tk.Label(control_panel, text="Threshold:")
        self.threshold_label.pack(side=tk.LEFT)

        self.threshold_entry = tk.Entry(control_panel, width=5)
        self.threshold_entry.pack(side=tk.LEFT)
        self.threshold_entry.insert(0, '5')  # Default threshold value
        self.threshold_entry.bind("<Return>", self.update_threshold)

        # Available filters
        self.filters = ["None", "Gaussian", "Mean", "Median", "Bilateral Filtering",
                    "Non-local Means Denoising", "Anisotropic Diffusion",
                    "Total Variation Denoising", "Wiener Filter",
                    "Adaptive Thresholding", "Haar Wavelet Transform",
                    "Daubechies Wavelet Transform"]

        # Subframe for complex controls such as combobox
        filter_frame = tk.Frame(control_panel)
        filter_frame.pack(side=tk.LEFT, fill=tk.X, expand=True)

        # Combobox for Selecting Filters
        self.filter_combobox = ttk.Combobox(filter_frame, values=self.filters)
        self.filter_combobox.pack(side=tk.LEFT, padx=10, pady=5)
        self.filter_combobox.current(0)  # Set default value

    def update_threshold(self, event):
        try:
            self.threshold = int(self.threshold_entry.get())
            print(f"Threshold updated to {self.threshold}")
        except ValueError:
            print("Invalid input for threshold. Please enter an integer.")

    def open_video(self):
        video_path = filedialog.askopenfilename(filetypes=[("Video files",
"*.mp4;*.avi;*.mkv;*.wmv")])
        if video_path:
            self.video = imageio.get_reader(video_path)
            self.frame_index = 0
            self.previous_frame = None
            self.paused = False
```

```python
            self.play_video()
            self.update_frame_label()

    def toggle_play_pause(self):
        self.paused = not self.paused
        if not self.paused:
            self.play_video()

    def stop_video(self):
        self.paused = True
        self.frame_index = 0
        self.previous_frame = None
        self.update_frame_label()
        self.display_frame(None)  # Clear the canvas

    def play_video(self):
        if not self.paused and self.video:
            if self.frame_index < len(self.video):
                try:
                    frame_data = self.video.get_data(self.frame_index)
                    frame = cv2.cvtColor(frame_data, cv2.COLOR_RGB2BGR)
                    self.process_frame(frame)
                    self.frame_index += 1
                    self.master.after(42, self.play_video)  # Schedule next frame
                except IndexError:
                    print("Reached the end of the video.")
                    self.paused = True  # Stop the video playback
                self.update_frame_label()

    def process_frame(self, frame):
        gray = cv2.cvtColor(frame, cv2.COLOR_BGR2GRAY)
        gray = cv2.GaussianBlur(gray, (21, 21), 0)
        if self.previous_frame is None:
            self.previous_frame = gray
            return

        frame_delta = cv2.absdiff(self.previous_frame, gray)
        thresh = cv2.threshold(frame_delta, self.threshold, 255, cv2.THRESH_BINARY)[1]
        thresh = cv2.dilate(thresh, None, iterations=2)
        contours, _ = cv2.findContours(thresh.copy(), cv2.RETR_EXTERNAL, cv2.CHAIN_APPROX_SIMPLE)

        self.listbox.delete(0, tk.END)  # Clear existing entries in the listbox
        box_number = 0  # Initialize box number
        for contour in contours:
            if cv2.contourArea(contour) < 500:
                continue
```

```python
                    box_number += 1  # Increment the box number for each contour
                    (x, y, w, h) = cv2.boundingRect(contour)
                    center_x, center_y = x + w // 2, y + h // 2
                    self.listbox.insert(tk.END, f"Box {box_number}: Center ({center_x}, {center_y})")
                    cv2.rectangle(frame, (x, y), (x+w, y+h), (50, 0, 255), 2)
                    cv2.putText(frame, f"{box_number}", (x + 5, y + 20), cv2.FONT_HERSHEY_SIMPLEX, 0.6, (0, 255, 0), 2)

        self.display_frame(frame)
        self.previous_frame = gray

    def display_frame(self, frame):
        if frame is not None:
            image = cv2.cvtColor(frame, cv2.COLOR_BGR2RGB)
            image = Image.fromarray(image)
            photo = ImageTk.PhotoImage(image=image)
            self.canvas.create_image(0, 0, anchor=tk.NW, image=photo)
            self.canvas.image = photo  # Keep the reference
        else:
            self.canvas.delete("all")

    def process_and_display_frame(self):
        if self.video and self.frame_index >= 0 and self.frame_index < len(self.video):
            try:
                frame_data = self.video.get_data(self.frame_index)
                frame = cv2.cvtColor(frame_data, cv2.COLOR_RGB2BGR)
                self.process_frame(frame)
            except IndexError:
                print(f"Frame index {self.frame_index} is out of range.")
                self.paused = True  # Pause to prevent further errors
            except Exception as e:
                print(f"Error processing frame: {e}")
                self.paused = True
            self.update_frame_label()

    def next_frame(self):
        if self.video and self.frame_index < len(self.video) - 1:  # Check if next frame exists
            self.frame_index += 1
            self.process_and_display_frame()
        else:
            print("No more frames to display.")
            self.paused = True

    def prev_frame(self):
        if self.video and self.frame_index > 0:
```

```python
            self.frame_index -= 1
            self.process_and_display_frame()
        else:
            print("Already at the first frame.")
            self.paused = True

def update_frame_label(self):
    self.frame_label.config(text=f"Frame: {self.frame_index}")

def on_mousewheel(self, event):
    direction = event.delta // 120
    current_value = int(self.zoom_scale.get())
    if direction == 1 and current_value < 10:
        current_value += 1
    elif direction == -1 and current_value > 1:
        current_value -= 1
    self.zoom_scale.set(current_value)
    self.update_zoom()

def on_press(self, event):
    self.tracker = None
    self.start_x = self.canvas.canvasx(event.x)
    self.start_y = self.canvas.canvasy(event.y)
    # Clear the previous bounding box if it exists
    if self.bbox_rect:
        self.canvas.delete(self.bbox_rect)
        self.bbox_rect = None
    self.bbox = None
    self.bbox2 = None

def on_drag(self, event):
    # Update the endpoint of the rectangle as the mouse moves
    cur_x = self.canvas.canvasx(event.x)
    cur_y = self.canvas.canvasy(event.y)

    # Define the coordinates correctly ensuring x1 < x2 and y1 < y2
    x1, y1 = min(self.start_x, cur_x), min(self.start_y, cur_y)
    x2, y2 = max(self.start_x, cur_x), max(self.start_y, cur_y)

    # Update dimensions for tracking
    self.initial_w = x2 - x1
    self.initial_h = y2 - y1
    self.bbox = (x1, y1, self.initial_w, self.initial_h)
    self.bbox2 = (self.start_x, self.start_y, cur_x, cur_y)

    # Update or create a rectangle on the canvas
    if self.bbox_rect:
        self.canvas.coords(self.bbox_rect, x1, y1, x2, y2)
```

```python
        else:
            self.bbox_rect = self.canvas.create_rectangle(x1, y1, x2, y2, 
outline="cyan", width=6)

    def on_release(self, event):
        self.analyze_histogram()  # Call analyze_histogram() method when the mouse 
button is released

    def analyze_histogram(self):
        if self.bbox2 is not None and self.video:
            x1, y1, x2, y2 = map(int, self.bbox2)
            if x1 != x2 and y1 != y2:
                try:
                    frame = self.video.get_data(self.frame_index)
                    # Ensure the bounding box is within the frame boundaries
                    h, w, _ = frame.shape
                    x1, x2 = max(0, min(x1, w)), max(0, min(x2, w))
                    y1, y2 = max(0, min(y1, h)), max(0, min(y2, h))

                    # Ensure x1 < x2 and y1 < y2
                    x1, x2 = sorted([x1, x2])
                    y1, y2 = sorted([y1, y2])

                    cropped_frame = frame[y1:y2, x1:x2]
                    if cropped_frame.size > 0:
                        cropped_frame = cv2.cvtColor(cropped_frame, 
cv2.COLOR_BGR2RGB)

                        # Get selected filter from combobox
                        selected_filter = self.filter_combobox.get()
                        # Apply selected filter
                        filtered_frame = self.apply_filter(selected_filter, 
cropped_frame)

                        self.create_popup_window(filtered_frame)
                        self.display_cropped_image(filtered_frame)
                        self.display_histograms(filtered_frame)
                    else:
                        print("Cropped frame is empty.")
                except Exception as e:
                    print("Failed to process frame:", e)
            else:
                print("Bounding box dimensions are zero or negative.")

    def create_popup_window(self, cropped_frame):
        self.popup_window = tk.Toplevel(self.master)
        self.popup_window.title("Cropped Image and Its Histogram")
        self.popup_window.geometry("1500x700")
```

```python
    def display_cropped_image(self, cropped_frame):
        cropped_frame_frame = tk.Frame(self.popup_window)
        cropped_frame_frame.pack(side="left")

        cropped_frame_rgb = cv2.cvtColor(cropped_frame, cv2.COLOR_BGR2RGB)
        cropped_img = Image.fromarray(cropped_frame_rgb)
        cropped_img = cropped_img.resize((600, 600))

        cropped_photo = ImageTk.PhotoImage(cropped_img)
        cropped_canvas = tk.Canvas(cropped_frame_frame, width=600, height=600)
        cropped_canvas.pack(side="left", anchor="nw")
        cropped_canvas.create_image(0, 0, anchor="nw", image=cropped_photo)
        cropped_canvas.image = cropped_photo

    def display_histograms(self, cropped_frame):
        histograms_frame = tk.Frame(self.popup_window)
        histograms_frame.pack(side="right", padx=20)

        self.display_line_histogram(cropped_frame, histograms_frame)
        self.display_bar_histogram(cropped_frame, histograms_frame)

    def display_line_histogram(self, cropped_frame, histograms_frame):
        line_histogram_frame = tk.Frame(histograms_frame)
        line_histogram_frame.pack(side="top", pady=10)

        plt.figure(figsize=(12, 4))
        color = ('r', 'g', 'b')
        for i, col in enumerate(color):
            histr = cv2.calcHist([cropped_frame], [i], None, [256], [0, 256])
            plt.plot(histr, color=col, label=f'Channel {col.upper()}', linewidth=2)
            plt.xlim([0, 256])
        plt.title('Line Histogram')
        plt.xlabel('Pixel Value')
        plt.ylabel('Frequency')
        plt.tight_layout()
        plt.grid(True)
        plt.legend()

        line_histogram_img = self.plot_to_image(plt)
        self.display_histogram_image(line_histogram_frame, line_histogram_img)

    def display_bar_histogram(self, cropped_frame, histograms_frame):
        bar_histogram_frame = tk.Frame(histograms_frame)
        bar_histogram_frame.pack(side="bottom", pady=10)

        plt.figure(figsize=(12, 4))
        color = ('r', 'g', 'b')
```

```python
        for i, col in enumerate(color):
            hist_range = (0, 256)
            hist_counts, _ = np.histogram(cropped_frame[:, :, i], bins=64, range=hist_range)
            plt.bar(np.arange(64), hist_counts, color=col, alpha=0.7, label=f'Channel {col.upper()}')
            for index, value in enumerate(hist_counts):
                plt.text(index, value + 10, str(int(value)), ha='center', va='bottom', fontsize=9)

        plt.title('Bar Histogram')
        plt.xlabel('Pixel Value')
        plt.ylabel('Frequency')
        plt.xticks(np.linspace(0, 63, num=5), np.linspace(0, 255, num=5, dtype=int))  # Adjust x-axis ticks
        plt.tight_layout()
        plt.grid(True)
        plt.legend()

        bar_histogram_img = self.plot_to_image(plt)
        self.display_histogram_image(bar_histogram_frame, bar_histogram_img)

    def display_histogram_image(self, parent_frame, img):
        histogram_photo = ImageTk.PhotoImage(image=img)
        histogram_canvas = tk.Canvas(parent_frame, width=900, height=300)
        histogram_canvas.pack(side="bottom", anchor="se")
        histogram_canvas.create_image(0, 0, anchor="nw", image=histogram_photo)
        histogram_canvas.image = histogram_photo

    def plot_histogram_bar_to_image(self, image):
        # Calculate histogram for each channel
        histograms = []
        for i in range(3):
            hist_range = (0, 256)
            hist_counts, _ = np.histogram(image[:, :, i], bins=64, range=hist_range)  # Adjust bins to 64
            histograms.append(hist_counts)

        # Extracting only 64 bins from the histogram
        num_bins = 64  # Adjusted to 64 bins

        # Generating colors for each channel
        colors = ['red', 'green', 'blue']

        plt.figure()
        for i, histogram in enumerate(histograms):
            # Normalize the histogram counts for better visualization
            hist_counts = histogram / np.sum(histogram)
```

```python
            # Setting the color for each channel
            plt.bar(np.arange(num_bins), hist_counts[:num_bins], color=colors[i], alpha=0.7, label=f'Channel {["Red", "Green", "Blue"][i]}')

        plt.xlabel('Pixel Value')
        plt.ylabel('Normalized Frequency')
        plt.title('RGB Channel Histograms')
        plt.grid(True)
        plt.tight_layout()
        plt.legend()

        # Convert the histogram bar graph to an image
        histogram_bar_img = self.plot_to_image(plt)
        histogram_bar_photo = ImageTk.PhotoImage(image=histogram_bar_img)

        return histogram_bar_photo

    def plot_to_image(self, plt):
        plt.savefig('temp_plot.png')
        img = Image.open('temp_plot.png')
        return img

    def apply_filter(self, filter_name, frame):
        if filter_name == "None":
            return frame
        elif filter_name == "Gaussian":
            return cv2.GaussianBlur(frame, (5, 5), 0)
        elif filter_name == "Mean":
            return cv2.blur(frame, (5, 5))
        elif filter_name == "Median":
            return cv2.medianBlur(frame, 5)
        elif filter_name == "Bilateral Filtering":
            return cv2.bilateralFilter(frame, 9, 75, 75)
        elif filter_name == "Non-local Means Denoising":
            return cv2.fastNlMeansDenoisingColored(frame, None, 10, 10, 7, 21)
        elif filter_name == "Anisotropic Diffusion":
            return self.anisotropic_diffusion(frame)
        elif filter_name == "Total Variation Denoising":
            return self.total_variation_denoising(frame)
        elif filter_name == "Wiener Filter":
            return self.wiener_filter(frame)
        elif filter_name == "Adaptive Thresholding":
            return self.adaptive_threshold_each_channel(frame)
        elif filter_name == "Haar Wavelet Transform":
            return self.haar_wavelet_transform(frame)
        elif filter_name == "Daubechies Wavelet Transform":
            return self.daubechies_wavelet_transform(frame)
        else:
```

```python
            return frame  # Default: return original frame if filter not found

    def wiener_filter(self, frame, kernel_size=(5, 5), noise_var=0.01):
        # Check if frame is None
        if frame is None:
            print("Error: Input frame is None.")
            return None

        # Check if frame is a valid numpy array
        if not isinstance(frame, np.ndarray):
            print("Error: Input frame is not a numpy array.")
            return None

        # Check if frame is an empty array
        if frame.size == 0:
            print("Error: Input frame is empty.")
            return None

        # Check if frame is in BGR color space
        if frame.shape[-1] != 3:
            print("Error: Input frame is not in BGR color space.")
            return None

        # Apply Wiener filter
        filtered_frame = cv2.medianBlur(frame, kernel_size[0])  # Use kernel_size[0] as the kernel size
        filtered_frame = cv2.fastNlMeansDenoising(filtered_frame, h=noise_var)
        return filtered_frame

    def adaptive_threshold_each_channel(self, frame):
        # Split the frame into individual channels
        b, g, r = cv2.split(frame)

        # Apply adaptive thresholding to each channel separately
        b_thresh = cv2.adaptiveThreshold(b, 255, cv2.ADAPTIVE_THRESH_GAUSSIAN_C, cv2.THRESH_BINARY, 11, 2)
        g_thresh = cv2.adaptiveThreshold(g, 255, cv2.ADAPTIVE_THRESH_GAUSSIAN_C, cv2.THRESH_BINARY, 11, 2)
        r_thresh = cv2.adaptiveThreshold(r, 255, cv2.ADAPTIVE_THRESH_GAUSSIAN_C, cv2.THRESH_BINARY, 11, 2)

        # Merge the thresholded channels back together
        return cv2.merge([b_thresh, g_thresh, r_thresh])

    def haar_wavelet_transform(self, frame):
        # Split the frame into its individual color channels
        b, g, r = cv2.split(frame)
```

```python
        # Perform the wavelet transform on each channel separately
        b_coeffs = pywt.dwt2(b, 'haar')
        g_coeffs = pywt.dwt2(g, 'haar')
        r_coeffs = pywt.dwt2(r, 'haar')

        # Reconstruct the channels from the coefficients
        b_reconstructed = pywt.idwt2(b_coeffs, 'haar')
        g_reconstructed = pywt.idwt2(g_coeffs, 'haar')
        r_reconstructed = pywt.idwt2(r_coeffs, 'haar')

        # Clip the values to ensure they are within the valid range
        b_reconstructed = np.clip(b_reconstructed, 0, 255).astype(np.uint8)
        g_reconstructed = np.clip(g_reconstructed, 0, 255).astype(np.uint8)
        r_reconstructed = np.clip(r_reconstructed, 0, 255).astype(np.uint8)

        # Merge the channels back together
        return cv2.merge([b_reconstructed, g_reconstructed, r_reconstructed])

    def daubechies_wavelet_transform(self, frame):
        # Split the frame into its individual color channels
        b, g, r = cv2.split(frame)

        # Choose the wavelet function (Daubechies 5)
        wavelet = 'db5'

        # Perform the wavelet transform on each channel separately
        b_coeffs = pywt.dwt2(b, wavelet)
        g_coeffs = pywt.dwt2(g, wavelet)
        r_coeffs = pywt.dwt2(r, wavelet)

        # Reconstruct the channels from the coefficients
        b_reconstructed = pywt.idwt2(b_coeffs, wavelet)
        g_reconstructed = pywt.idwt2(g_coeffs, wavelet)
        r_reconstructed = pywt.idwt2(r_coeffs, wavelet)

        # Clip the values to ensure they are within the valid range
        b_reconstructed = np.clip(b_reconstructed, 0, 255).astype(np.uint8)
        g_reconstructed = np.clip(g_reconstructed, 0, 255).astype(np.uint8)
        r_reconstructed = np.clip(r_reconstructed, 0, 255).astype(np.uint8)

        # Merge the channels back together
        return cv2.merge([b_reconstructed, g_reconstructed, r_reconstructed])

    def anisotropic_diffusion(self, img):
        return cv2.fastNlMeansDenoisingColored(img, None, 10, 10, 7, 21)

    def apply_total_variation_denoising_channel(self, channel, weight, iterations):
        # Initialize the result with the original channel
```

```python
            result = channel.copy().astype(np.float64)  # Convert to float64

            # Perform total variation denoising
            for _ in range(iterations):
                # Compute the gradient of the channel
                dx = cv2.Sobel(result, cv2.CV_64F, 1, 0, ksize=3)
                dy = cv2.Sobel(result, cv2.CV_64F, 0, 1, ksize=3)

                # Update the channel using the gradient and the weight
                result -= weight * np.sqrt(dx**2 + dy**2)

            # Clip the values to ensure they are within the valid range
            result = np.clip(result, 0, 255).astype(np.uint8)

            return result

    def total_variation_denoising(self, img, weight=0.01, iterations=20):
        # Split the image into its individual color channels
        b, g, r = cv2.split(img)

        # Apply total variation denoising to each channel separately
        b_denoised = self.apply_total_variation_denoising_channel(b, weight, iterations)
        g_denoised = self.apply_total_variation_denoising_channel(g, weight, iterations)
        r_denoised = self.apply_total_variation_denoising_channel(r, weight, iterations)

        # Merge the denoised channels back together
        return cv2.merge([b_denoised, g_denoised, r_denoised])

def main():
    root = tk.Tk()
    app = FrameDifferencer(root)
    root.mainloop()

if __name__ == "__main__":
    main()
```

MOTION DETECTION WITH RUNNING GAUSSIAN AVERAGE

DESCRIPTION

The project defines a class RunningGaussianAverage designed to implement motion detection using a running Gaussian average technique within a graphical user interface (GUI) based on Tkinter. The class is structured to initialize with a master window and includes methods for interacting with video files, processing the frames for motion detection, and displaying both the frames and motion-related information.

Upon initialization, the RunningGaussianAverage class sets the title of the master window and initializes several variables for video processing, including placeholders for the video stream, the previous frame, the running average of frames, and various control flags like whether the video is paused. It also sets up the initial threshold for detecting significant changes in the video frames. This setup is accompanied by creating widgets such as buttons, a canvas for displaying video, and a listbox for listing detected motion centers, providing a complete GUI environment.

The create_widgets() method within the class organizes the GUI layout. This method establishes a main display area with a canvas to show video frames and a listbox to display detections. Additionally, a control panel contains buttons to open and control video playback, such as play, pause, stop, and navigate through frames. This structure allows users to interactively manage video playback and observe the application's output directly.

For handling video, methods like open_video(), toggle_play_pause(), and play_video() allow users to load a video file, start or pause playback, and continuously display video frames, respectively. These functions integrate with the imageio library for reading video files, making the application capable of handling common video formats.

The core functionality revolves around the process_frame method, which applies a running Gaussian average to detect motion. This method calculates the difference between the current frame and a running average, which is updated continuously, to highlight areas of significant change. It uses OpenCV functions for image processing tasks such as converting to grayscale, blurring, and thresholding to detect motion. Detected changes are then visually marked and listed in the GUI for user reference.

Finally, the script contains a main function to create the root window and run the application, ensuring that the GUI event loop starts when the script is executed directly. This setup ensures that the application is ready to be used immediately after launching, providing an intuitive and interactive tool for motion detection using video input.

PROCESSING FRAME

```python
    def process_frame(self, frame):
        gray = cv2.cvtColor(frame, cv2.COLOR_BGR2GRAY)
        gray = cv2.GaussianBlur(gray, (21, 21), 0)  # Blur to reduce noise

        if self.running_average is None:
            self.running_average = gray.astype("float")
            return  # Skip the rest until the running average is initialized

        # Update the running average
        cv2.accumulateWeighted(gray, self.running_average, 0.05)

        # Compute the difference between the current frame and the running average
        frame_delta = cv2.absdiff(gray, cv2.convertScaleAbs(self.running_average))

        # Threshold the delta image
        thresh = cv2.threshold(frame_delta, self.threshold, 255, cv2.THRESH_BINARY)[1]
        thresh = cv2.dilate(thresh, None, iterations=2)  # Dilate the thresholded image to fill in holes

        # Find contours on the thresholded image
        contours, _ = cv2.findContours(thresh.copy(), cv2.RETR_EXTERNAL, cv2.CHAIN_APPROX_SIMPLE)

        self.listbox.delete(0, tk.END)  # Clear existing entries in the listbox
        box_number = 0  # Initialize box number

        # Loop over the contours
        for contour in contours:
            if cv2.contourArea(contour) < 500:
                continue  # Ignore small contours
            box_number += 1  # Increment the box number for each contour
            (x, y, w, h) = cv2.boundingRect(contour)
            center_x, center_y = x + w // 2, y + h // 2
            cv2.rectangle(frame, (x, y), (x+w, y+h), (50, 0, 255), 2)
            self.listbox.insert(tk.END, f"Box {box_number}: Center ({center_x}, {center_y})")
            cv2.rectangle(frame, (x, y), (x+w, y+h), (50, 0, 255), 2)
            cv2.putText(frame, f"{box_number}", (x + 5, y + 20), cv2.FONT_HERSHEY_SIMPLEX, 0.6, (0, 255, 0), 2)
        self.display_frame(frame)
```

The process_frame() method in the RunningGaussianAverage class is an essential component of the application, specifically designed to detect motion by analyzing video frames against a running average. This method combines various OpenCV functions to process video data and visualize the results. Here's a detailed breakdown of each step within this method:

1. Convert to Grayscale:

   The method begins by converting the input color frame (BGR format) to grayscale using cv2.cvtColor. Grayscale conversion is a common first step in motion detection algorithms because it simplifies the analysis by reducing the dimensionality of the image data (from three color channels to one).

2. Apply Gaussian Blur:

   Next, the frame is blurred using Gaussian Blur (cv2.GaussianBlur) with a kernel size of (21, 21). Blurring helps to reduce noise and detail in the image, which can improve the robustness of motion detection by smoothing out irrelevant variations and emphasizing significant changes.

3. Initialize or Update Running Average:
   - If self.running_average is None (indicating the first frame or reset), it initializes this running average with the current gray frame converted to a floating-point format. This initialization is crucial as the running average needs a starting point.
   - If already initialized, cv2.accumulateWeighted is used to update the running average with the new frame. This function computes a weighted average of the input image and the accumulated background model to produce a running average image that adapts over time. The weight (0.05 here) determines how quickly the model adapts to changes in the scene.

4. Compute Frame Difference:

   The method computes the absolute difference between the current gray frame and the running average using cv2.absdiff. The running average serves as a background model, and the difference highlights regions with significant deviations from this model, indicating potential motion.

5. Threshold and Dilate:
   - A binary threshold is applied to the frame difference to create a binary image where the regions of significant change are white (motion detected) and all else is black. This is done using cv2.threshold.
   - The thresholded image is then dilated using cv2.dilate to fill in holes and expand the areas marked as motion. Dilation helps connect contiguous areas and smooth the shapes of detected regions.

6. Detect and Process Contours:
   - cv2.findContours is used to extract contours from the dilated image. Contours are used to outline the continuous regions in the binary image, effectively identifying individual movements or changes in the scene.
   - The method iterates over each contour, filtering out small ones (less than 500 pixels in area) to ignore minor changes or noise. For each significant contour, a bounding rectangle is calculated, and details about the detected motion (like the center coordinates) are added to a listbox for display.

7. Display Updated Frame:
   - Each detected motion region is visually highlighted on the frame by drawing rectangles and labels around them. This helps users visually verify where motion was detected in the video.
   - Finally, the processed frame is displayed in the GUI using the self.display_frame(frame) method, which updates the canvas with the new frame.

Overall, this method effectively integrates frame processing with graphical updates, providing a robust system for real-time motion detection in video streams. It leverages OpenCV's powerful image processing capabilities to perform tasks essential for detecting and visualizing motion, making it suitable for applications like surveillance, activity monitoring, or automated video analysis.

RUNNING PROGRAM

Run program and click on Play/Pause button. Or, you can choose certain frame by pushing Next Frame button. Then, draw a bounding box rectangle on certain object in the frame and push Next Frame button.

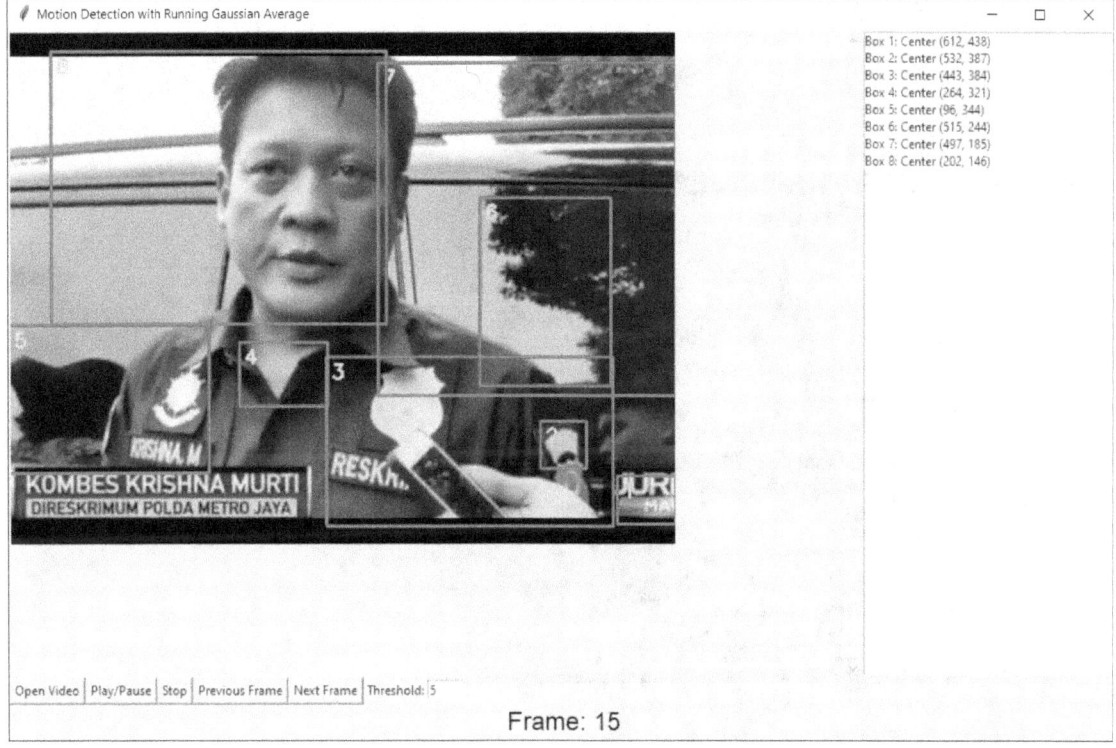

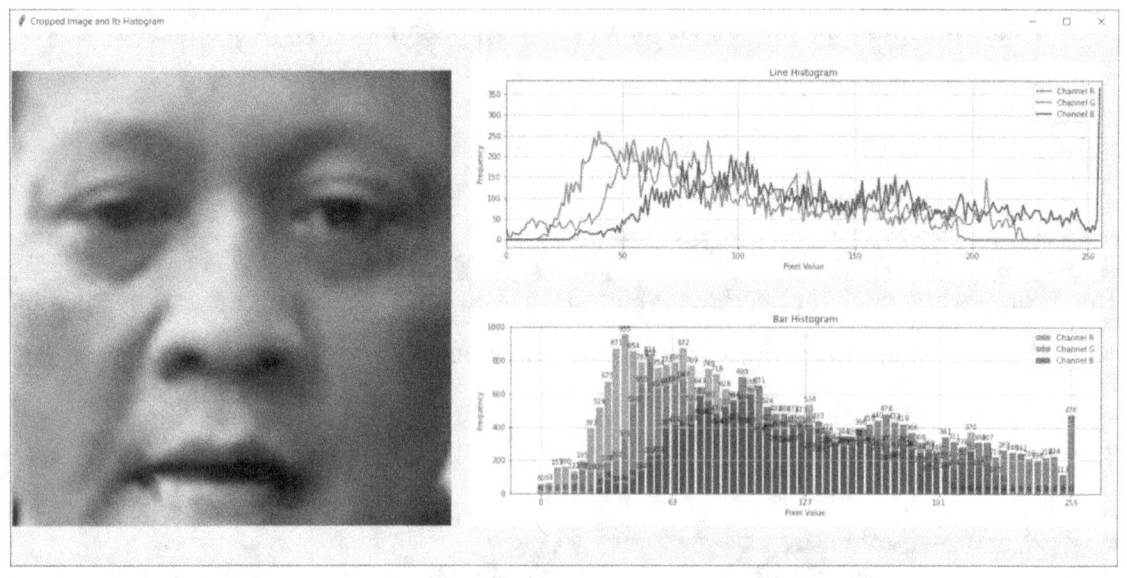

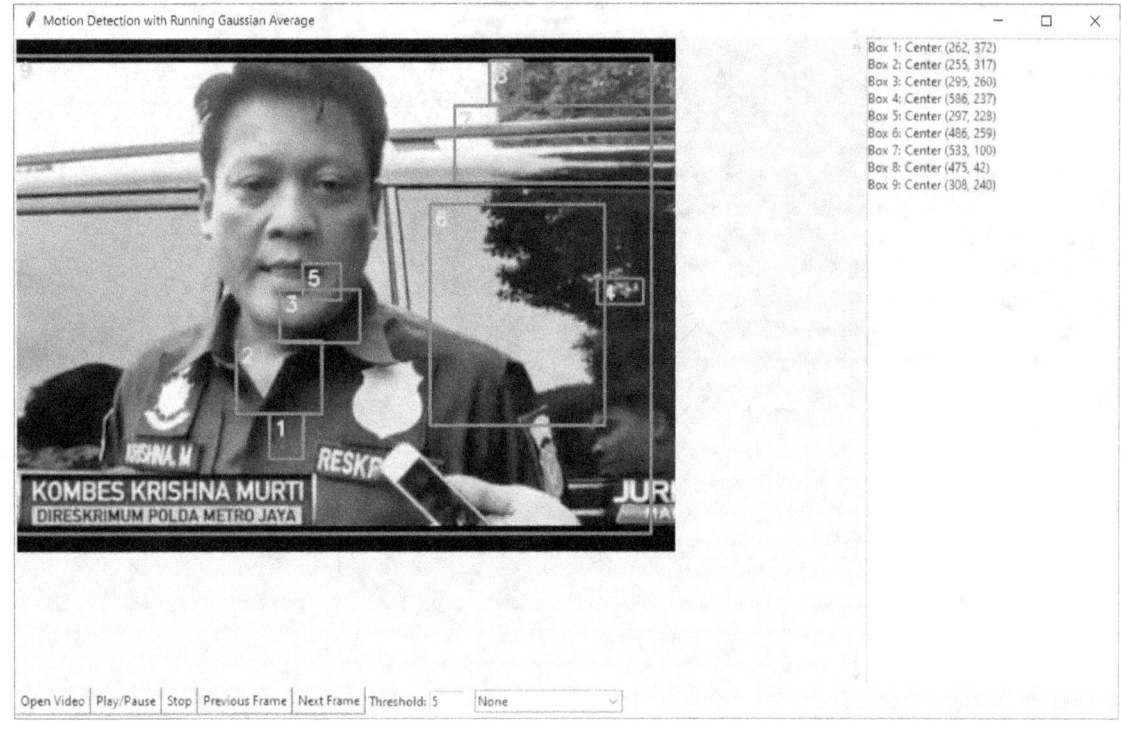

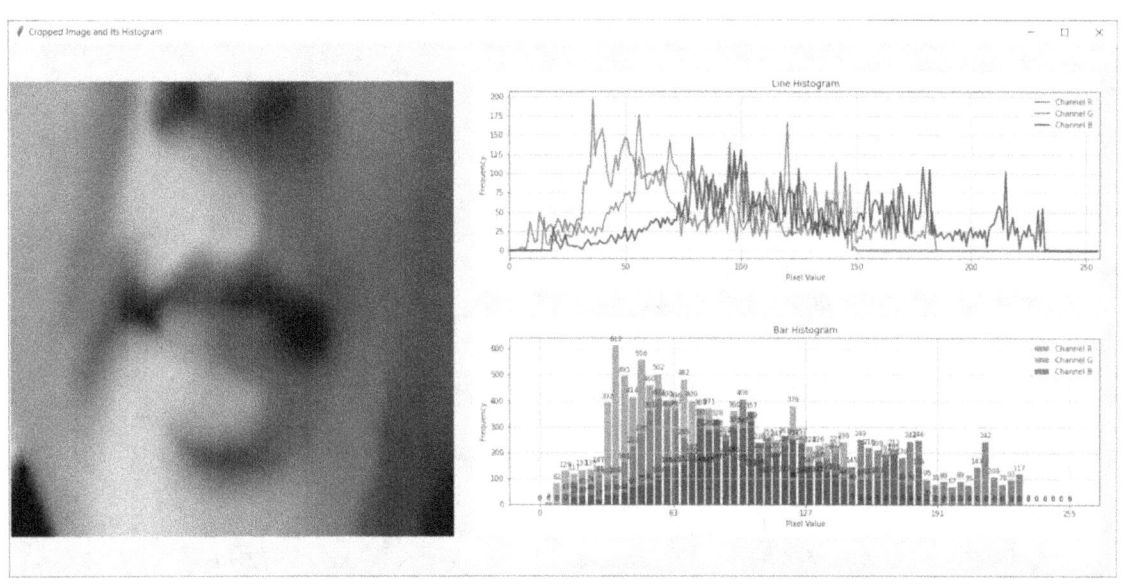

SOURCE CODE

```
#running_gaussian_average_with_filtering.py
import tkinter as tk
from tkinter import ttk
from tkinter import filedialog
from PIL import Image, ImageTk
import cv2
import imageio
import matplotlib.pyplot as plt
import pywt
import numpy as np

class RunningGaussianAverage:
    def __init__(self, master):
        self.master = master
        self.master.title("Motion Detection with Running Gaussian Average")
        self.bbox_rect = None  # Initialize bbox_rect attribute to None
        self.running_average = None  # Stores the running average of frames

        # Video related variables
        self.video = None
        self.previous_frame = None
        self.frame_index = 0
        self.paused = True
```

```python
        self.threshold = 5  # Default threshold for frame differencing

        # Creates widgets
        self.create_widgets(master)

    def create_widgets(self, master):
        # Create a frame for the canvas and listbox
        display_frame = tk.Frame(master)
        display_frame.pack(fill=tk.BOTH, expand=True)

        # Set up the canvas
        self.canvas = tk.Canvas(display_frame, width=800, height=600)
        self.canvas.pack(side=tk.LEFT, fill=tk.BOTH, expand=True)
        self.canvas.bind("<MouseWheel>", self.on_mousewheel)
        self.canvas.bind("<ButtonPress-1>", self.on_press)
        self.canvas.bind("<B1-Motion>", self.on_drag)
        self.canvas.bind("<ButtonRelease-1>", self.on_release)  # Bind ButtonRelease event

        # Set up the listbox for displaying centers
        self.listbox = tk.Listbox(display_frame, width=40, height=20)
        self.listbox.pack(side=tk.RIGHT, fill=tk.Y)

        # Add scrollbar to the listbox
        scrollbar = tk.Scrollbar(display_frame, orient="vertical", command=self.listbox.yview)
        scrollbar.pack(side=tk.RIGHT, fill=tk.Y)
        self.listbox.config(yscrollcommand=scrollbar.set)

        # Control Panel below the display frame
        control_panel = tk.Frame(master)
        control_panel.pack(fill=tk.X)

        self.open_button = tk.Button(control_panel, text="Open Video", command=self.open_video)
        self.open_button.pack(side=tk.LEFT)

        self.play_button = tk.Button(control_panel, text="Play/Pause", command=self.toggle_play_pause)
        self.play_button.pack(side=tk.LEFT)

        self.stop_button = tk.Button(control_panel, text="Stop", command=self.stop_video)
        self.stop_button.pack(side=tk.LEFT)

        self.prev_button = tk.Button(control_panel, text="Previous Frame", command=self.prev_frame)
        self.prev_button.pack(side=tk.LEFT)
```

```python
        self.next_button = tk.Button(control_panel, text="Next Frame", 
command=self.next_frame)
        self.next_button.pack(side=tk.LEFT)
        
        # Threshold Control
        self.threshold_label = tk.Label(control_panel, text="Threshold:")
        self.threshold_label.pack(side=tk.LEFT)

        self.threshold_entry = tk.Entry(control_panel, width=5)
        self.threshold_entry.pack(side=tk.LEFT)
        self.threshold_entry.insert(0, '5')  # Default threshold value
        self.threshold_entry.bind("<Return>", self.update_threshold)

        # Available filters
        self.filters = ["None", "Gaussian", "Mean", "Median", "Bilateral Filtering",
                        "Non-local Means Denoising", "Anisotropic Diffusion",
                        "Total Variation Denoising", "Wiener Filter",
                        "Adaptive Thresholding", "Haar Wavelet Transform",
                        "Daubechies Wavelet Transform"]

        # Subframe for complex controls such as combobox
        filter_frame = tk.Frame(control_panel)
        filter_frame.pack(side=tk.LEFT, fill=tk.X, expand=True)

        # Combobox for Selecting Filters
        self.filter_combobox = ttk.Combobox(filter_frame, values=self.filters)
        self.filter_combobox.pack(side=tk.LEFT, padx=10, pady=5)
        self.filter_combobox.current(0)  # Set default value

    def update_threshold(self, event):
        try:
            self.threshold = int(self.threshold_entry.get())
            print(f"Threshold updated to {self.threshold}")
        except ValueError:
            print("Invalid input for threshold. Please enter an integer.")

    def open_video(self):
        video_path = filedialog.askopenfilename(filetypes=[("Video files",
"*.mp4;*.avi;*.mkv;*.wmv")])
        if video_path:
            self.video = imageio.get_reader(video_path)
            self.frame_index = 0
            self.previous_frame = None
            self.paused = False
            self.play_video()
            self.update_frame_label()
```

```python
    def toggle_play_pause(self):
        self.paused = not self.paused
        if not self.paused:
            self.play_video()

    def stop_video(self):
        self.paused = True
        self.frame_index = 0
        self.previous_frame = None
        self.update_frame_label()
        self.display_frame(None)  # Clear the canvas

    def play_video(self):
        if not self.paused and self.video:
            if self.frame_index < len(self.video):
                try:
                    frame_data = self.video.get_data(self.frame_index)
                    frame = cv2.cvtColor(frame_data, cv2.COLOR_RGB2BGR)
                    self.process_frame(frame)
                    self.frame_index += 1
                    self.master.after(42, self.play_video)  # Schedule next frame
                except IndexError:
                    print("Reached the end of the video.")
                    self.paused = True  # Stop the video playback
                self.update_frame_label()

    def process_frame(self, frame):
        gray = cv2.cvtColor(frame, cv2.COLOR_BGR2GRAY)
        gray = cv2.GaussianBlur(gray, (21, 21), 0)  # Blur to reduce noise

        if self.running_average is None:
            self.running_average = gray.astype("float")
            return  # Skip the rest until the running average is initialized

        # Update the running average
        cv2.accumulateWeighted(gray, self.running_average, 0.05)

        # Compute the difference between the current frame and the running average
        frame_delta = cv2.absdiff(gray, cv2.convertScaleAbs(self.running_average))

        # Threshold the delta image
        thresh = cv2.threshold(frame_delta, self.threshold, 255,
cv2.THRESH_BINARY)[1]
        thresh = cv2.dilate(thresh, None, iterations=2)  # Dilate the thresholded
image to fill in holes

        # Find contours on the thresholded image
```

```python
            contours, _ = cv2.findContours(thresh.copy(), cv2.RETR_EXTERNAL, 
cv2.CHAIN_APPROX_SIMPLE)

            self.listbox.delete(0, tk.END)  # Clear existing entries in the listbox
            box_number = 0  # Initialize box number

            # Loop over the contours
            for contour in contours:
                if cv2.contourArea(contour) < 500:
                    continue  # Ignore small contours
                box_number += 1  # Increment the box number for each contour
                (x, y, w, h) = cv2.boundingRect(contour)
                center_x, center_y = x + w // 2, y + h // 2
                cv2.rectangle(frame, (x, y), (x+w, y+h), (50, 0, 255), 2)
                self.listbox.insert(tk.END, f"Box {box_number}: Center ({center_x}, 
{center_y})")
                cv2.rectangle(frame, (x, y), (x+w, y+h), (50, 0, 255), 2)
                cv2.putText(frame, f"{box_number}", (x + 5, y + 20), 
cv2.FONT_HERSHEY_SIMPLEX, 0.6, (0, 255, 0), 2)
            self.display_frame(frame)

    def display_frame(self, frame):
        if frame is not None:
            image = cv2.cvtColor(frame, cv2.COLOR_BGR2RGB)
            image = Image.fromarray(image)
            photo = ImageTk.PhotoImage(image=image)
            self.canvas.create_image(0, 0, anchor=tk.NW, image=photo)
            self.canvas.image = photo  # Keep the reference
        else:
            self.canvas.delete("all")

    def process_and_display_frame(self):
        if self.video and self.frame_index >= 0 and self.frame_index < 
len(self.video):
            try:
                frame_data = self.video.get_data(self.frame_index)
                frame = cv2.cvtColor(frame_data, cv2.COLOR_RGB2BGR)
                self.process_frame(frame)
            except IndexError:
                print(f"Frame index {self.frame_index} is out of range.")
                self.paused = True  # Pause to prevent further errors
            except Exception as e:
                print(f"Error processing frame: {e}")
                self.paused = True
            self.update_frame_label()

    def next_frame(self):
```

```python
        if self.video and self.frame_index < len(self.video) - 1:  # Check if next frame exists
            self.frame_index += 1
            self.process_and_display_frame()
        else:
            print("No more frames to display.")
            self.paused = True

    def prev_frame(self):
        if self.video and self.frame_index > 0:
            self.frame_index -= 1
            self.process_and_display_frame()
        else:
            print("Already at the first frame.")
            self.paused = True


    def update_frame_label(self):
        self.frame_label.config(text=f"Frame: {self.frame_index}")

    def on_mousewheel(self, event):
        direction = event.delta // 120
        current_value = int(self.zoom_scale.get())
        if direction == 1 and current_value < 10:
            current_value += 1
        elif direction == -1 and current_value > 1:
            current_value -= 1
        self.zoom_scale.set(current_value)
        self.update_zoom()

    def on_press(self, event):
        self.tracker = None
        self.start_x = self.canvas.canvasx(event.x)
        self.start_y = self.canvas.canvasy(event.y)
        # Clear the previous bounding box if it exists
        if self.bbox_rect:
            self.canvas.delete(self.bbox_rect)
            self.bbox_rect = None
        self.bbox = None
        self.bbox2 = None

    def on_drag(self, event):
        # Update the endpoint of the rectangle as the mouse moves
        cur_x = self.canvas.canvasx(event.x)
        cur_y = self.canvas.canvasy(event.y)

        # Define the coordinates correctly ensuring x1 < x2 and y1 < y2
        x1, y1 = min(self.start_x, cur_x), min(self.start_y, cur_y)
```

```python
            x2, y2 = max(self.start_x, cur_x), max(self.start_y, cur_y)

            # Update dimensions for tracking
            self.initial_w = x2 - x1
            self.initial_h = y2 - y1
            self.bbox = (x1, y1, self.initial_w, self.initial_h)
            self.bbox2 = (self.start_x, self.start_y, cur_x, cur_y)

            # Update or create a rectangle on the canvas
            if self.bbox_rect:
                self.canvas.coords(self.bbox_rect, x1, y1, x2, y2)
            else:
                self.bbox_rect = self.canvas.create_rectangle(x1, y1, x2, y2, outline="cyan", width=6)

    def on_release(self, self, event):
        self.analyze_histogram()  # Call analyze_histogram() method when the mouse button is released

    def analyze_histogram(self):
        if self.bbox2 is not None and self.video:
            x1, y1, x2, y2 = map(int, self.bbox2)
            if x1 != x2 and y1 != y2:
                try:
                    frame = self.video.get_data(self.frame_index)
                    # Ensure the bounding box is within the frame boundaries
                    h, w, _ = frame.shape
                    x1, x2 = max(0, min(x1, w)), max(0, min(x2, w))
                    y1, y2 = max(0, min(y1, h)), max(0, min(y2, h))

                    # Ensure x1 < x2 and y1 < y2
                    x1, x2 = sorted([x1, x2])
                    y1, y2 = sorted([y1, y2])

                    cropped_frame = frame[y1:y2, x1:x2]
                    if cropped_frame.size > 0:
                        cropped_frame = cv2.cvtColor(cropped_frame, cv2.COLOR_BGR2RGB)

                        # Get selected filter from combobox
                        selected_filter = self.filter_combobox.get()
                        # Apply selected filter
                        filtered_frame = self.apply_filter(selected_filter, cropped_frame)

                        self.create_popup_window(filtered_frame)
                        self.display_cropped_image(filtered_frame)
                        self.display_histograms(filtered_frame)
```

```python
                    else:
                        print("Cropped frame is empty.")
                except Exception as e:
                    print("Failed to process frame:", e)
            else:
                print("Bounding box dimensions are zero or negative.")

    def create_popup_window(self, cropped_frame):
        self.popup_window = tk.Toplevel(self.master)
        self.popup_window.title("Cropped Image and Its Histogram")
        self.popup_window.geometry("1500x700")

    def display_cropped_image(self, cropped_frame):
        cropped_frame_frame = tk.Frame(self.popup_window)
        cropped_frame_frame.pack(side="left")

        cropped_frame_rgb = cv2.cvtColor(cropped_frame, cv2.COLOR_BGR2RGB)
        cropped_img = Image.fromarray(cropped_frame_rgb)
        cropped_img = cropped_img.resize((600, 600))

        cropped_photo = ImageTk.PhotoImage(cropped_img)
        cropped_canvas = tk.Canvas(cropped_frame_frame, width=600, height=600)
        cropped_canvas.pack(side="left", anchor="nw")
        cropped_canvas.create_image(0, 0, anchor="nw", image=cropped_photo)
        cropped_canvas.image = cropped_photo

    def display_histograms(self, cropped_frame):
        histograms_frame = tk.Frame(self.popup_window)
        histograms_frame.pack(side="right", padx=20)

        self.display_line_histogram(cropped_frame, histograms_frame)
        self.display_bar_histogram(cropped_frame, histograms_frame)

    def display_line_histogram(self, cropped_frame, histograms_frame):
        line_histogram_frame = tk.Frame(histograms_frame)
        line_histogram_frame.pack(side="top", pady=10)

        plt.figure(figsize=(12, 4))
        color = ('r', 'g', 'b')
        for i, col in enumerate(color):
            histr = cv2.calcHist([cropped_frame], [i], None, [256], [0, 256])
            plt.plot(histr, color=col, label=f'Channel {col.upper()}', linewidth=2)
            plt.xlim([0, 256])
        plt.title('Line Histogram')
        plt.xlabel('Pixel Value')
        plt.ylabel('Frequency')
```

```python
        plt.tight_layout()
        plt.grid(True)
        plt.legend()

        line_histogram_img = self.plot_to_image(plt)
        self.display_histogram_image(line_histogram_frame, line_histogram_img)

    def display_bar_histogram(self, cropped_frame, histograms_frame):
        bar_histogram_frame = tk.Frame(histograms_frame)
        bar_histogram_frame.pack(side="bottom", pady=10)

        plt.figure(figsize=(12, 4))
        color = ('r', 'g', 'b')
        for i, col in enumerate(color):
            hist_range = (0, 256)
            hist_counts, _ = np.histogram(cropped_frame[:, :, i], bins=64, range=hist_range)
            plt.bar(np.arange(64), hist_counts, color=col, alpha=0.7, label=f'Channel {col.upper()}')
            for index, value in enumerate(hist_counts):
                plt.text(index, value + 10, str(int(value)), ha='center', va='bottom', fontsize=9)

        plt.title('Bar Histogram')
        plt.xlabel('Pixel Value')
        plt.ylabel('Frequency')
        plt.xticks(np.linspace(0, 63, num=5), np.linspace(0, 255, num=5, dtype=int))  
        # Adjust x-axis ticks
        plt.tight_layout()
        plt.grid(True)
        plt.legend()

        bar_histogram_img = self.plot_to_image(plt)
        self.display_histogram_image(bar_histogram_frame, bar_histogram_img)

    def display_histogram_image(self, parent_frame, img):
        histogram_photo = ImageTk.PhotoImage(image=img)
        histogram_canvas = tk.Canvas(parent_frame, width=900, height=300)
        histogram_canvas.pack(side="bottom", anchor="se")
        histogram_canvas.create_image(0, 0, anchor="nw", image=histogram_photo)
        histogram_canvas.image = histogram_photo

    def plot_histogram_bar_to_image(self, image):
        # Calculate histogram for each channel
        histograms = []
        for i in range(3):
            hist_range = (0, 256)
```

```python
            hist_counts, _ = np.histogram(image[:, :, i], bins=64, range=hist_range)
# Adjust bins to 64
            histograms.append(hist_counts)

        # Extracting only 64 bins from the histogram
        num_bins = 64  # Adjusted to 64 bins

        # Generating colors for each channel
        colors = ['red', 'green', 'blue']

        plt.figure()
        for i, histogram in enumerate(histograms):
            # Normalize the histogram counts for better visualization
            hist_counts = histogram / np.sum(histogram)
            # Setting the color for each channel
            plt.bar(np.arange(num_bins), hist_counts[:num_bins], color=colors[i],
alpha=0.7, label=f'Channel {["Red", "Green", "Blue"][i]}')

        plt.xlabel('Pixel Value')
        plt.ylabel('Normalized Frequency')
        plt.title('RGB Channel Histograms')
        plt.grid(True)
        plt.tight_layout()
        plt.legend()

        # Convert the histogram bar graph to an image
        histogram_bar_img = self.plot_to_image(plt)
        histogram_bar_photo = ImageTk.PhotoImage(image=histogram_bar_img)

        return histogram_bar_photo

    def plot_to_image(self, plt):
        plt.savefig('temp_plot.png')
        img = Image.open('temp_plot.png')
        return img

    def apply_filter(self, filter_name, frame):
        if filter_name == "None":
            return frame
        elif filter_name == "Gaussian":
            return cv2.GaussianBlur(frame, (5, 5), 0)
        elif filter_name == "Mean":
            return cv2.blur(frame, (5, 5))
        elif filter_name == "Median":
            return cv2.medianBlur(frame, 5)
        elif filter_name == "Bilateral Filtering":
            return cv2.bilateralFilter(frame, 9, 75, 75)
        elif filter_name == "Non-local Means Denoising":
```

```python
            return cv2.fastNlMeansDenoisingColored(frame, None, 10, 10, 7, 21)
        elif filter_name == "Anisotropic Diffusion":
            return self.anisotropic_diffusion(frame)
        elif filter_name == "Total Variation Denoising":
            return self.total_variation_denoising(frame)
        elif filter_name == "Wiener Filter":
            return self.wiener_filter(frame)
        elif filter_name == "Adaptive Thresholding":
            return self.adaptive_threshold_each_channel(frame)
        elif filter_name == "Haar Wavelet Transform":
            return self.haar_wavelet_transform(frame)
        elif filter_name == "Daubechies Wavelet Transform":
            return self.daubechies_wavelet_transform(frame)
        else:
            return frame  # Default: return original frame if filter not found

    def wiener_filter(self, frame, kernel_size=(5, 5), noise_var=0.01):
        # Check if frame is None
        if frame is None:
            print("Error: Input frame is None.")
            return None

        # Check if frame is a valid numpy array
        if not isinstance(frame, np.ndarray):
            print("Error: Input frame is not a numpy array.")
            return None

        # Check if frame is an empty array
        if frame.size == 0:
            print("Error: Input frame is empty.")
            return None

        # Check if frame is in BGR color space
        if frame.shape[-1] != 3:
            print("Error: Input frame is not in BGR color space.")
            return None

        # Apply Wiener filter
        filtered_frame = cv2.medianBlur(frame, kernel_size[0])  # Use kernel_size[0] as the kernel size
        filtered_frame = cv2.fastNlMeansDenoising(filtered_frame, h=noise_var)
        return filtered_frame

    def adaptive_threshold_each_channel(self, frame):
        # Split the frame into individual channels
        b, g, r = cv2.split(frame)

        # Apply adaptive thresholding to each channel separately
```

```python
        b_thresh = cv2.adaptiveThreshold(b, 255, cv2.ADAPTIVE_THRESH_GAUSSIAN_C, 
cv2.THRESH_BINARY, 11, 2)
        g_thresh = cv2.adaptiveThreshold(g, 255, cv2.ADAPTIVE_THRESH_GAUSSIAN_C, 
cv2.THRESH_BINARY, 11, 2)
        r_thresh = cv2.adaptiveThreshold(r, 255, cv2.ADAPTIVE_THRESH_GAUSSIAN_C, 
cv2.THRESH_BINARY, 11, 2)

        # Merge the thresholded channels back together
        return cv2.merge([b_thresh, g_thresh, r_thresh])

    def haar_wavelet_transform(self, frame):
        # Split the frame into its individual color channels
        b, g, r = cv2.split(frame)

        # Perform the wavelet transform on each channel separately
        b_coeffs = pywt.dwt2(b, 'haar')
        g_coeffs = pywt.dwt2(g, 'haar')
        r_coeffs = pywt.dwt2(r, 'haar')

        # Reconstruct the channels from the coefficients
        b_reconstructed = pywt.idwt2(b_coeffs, 'haar')
        g_reconstructed = pywt.idwt2(g_coeffs, 'haar')
        r_reconstructed = pywt.idwt2(r_coeffs, 'haar')

        # Clip the values to ensure they are within the valid range
        b_reconstructed = np.clip(b_reconstructed, 0, 255).astype(np.uint8)
        g_reconstructed = np.clip(g_reconstructed, 0, 255).astype(np.uint8)
        r_reconstructed = np.clip(r_reconstructed, 0, 255).astype(np.uint8)

        # Merge the channels back together
        return cv2.merge([b_reconstructed, g_reconstructed, r_reconstructed])

    def daubechies_wavelet_transform(self, frame):
        # Split the frame into its individual color channels
        b, g, r = cv2.split(frame)

        # Choose the wavelet function (Daubechies 5)
        wavelet = 'db5'

        # Perform the wavelet transform on each channel separately
        b_coeffs = pywt.dwt2(b, wavelet)
        g_coeffs = pywt.dwt2(g, wavelet)
        r_coeffs = pywt.dwt2(r, wavelet)

        # Reconstruct the channels from the coefficients
        b_reconstructed = pywt.idwt2(b_coeffs, wavelet)
        g_reconstructed = pywt.idwt2(g_coeffs, wavelet)
        r_reconstructed = pywt.idwt2(r_coeffs, wavelet)
```

```python
        # Clip the values to ensure they are within the valid range
        b_reconstructed = np.clip(b_reconstructed, 0, 255).astype(np.uint8)
        g_reconstructed = np.clip(g_reconstructed, 0, 255).astype(np.uint8)
        r_reconstructed = np.clip(r_reconstructed, 0, 255).astype(np.uint8)

        # Merge the channels back together
        return cv2.merge([b_reconstructed, g_reconstructed, r_reconstructed])

    def anisotropic_diffusion(self, img):
        return cv2.fastNlMeansDenoisingColored(img, None, 10, 10, 7, 21)

    def apply_total_variation_denoising_channel(self, channel, weight, iterations):
        # Initialize the result with the original channel
        result = channel.copy().astype(np.float64)  # Convert to float64

        # Perform total variation denoising
        for _ in range(iterations):
            # Compute the gradient of the channel
            dx = cv2.Sobel(result, cv2.CV_64F, 1, 0, ksize=3)
            dy = cv2.Sobel(result, cv2.CV_64F, 0, 1, ksize=3)

            # Update the channel using the gradient and the weight
            result -= weight * np.sqrt(dx**2 + dy**2)

        # Clip the values to ensure they are within the valid range
        result = np.clip(result, 0, 255).astype(np.uint8)

        return result

    def total_variation_denoising(self, img, weight=0.01, iterations=20):
        # Split the image into its individual color channels
        b, g, r = cv2.split(img)

        # Apply total variation denoising to each channel separately
        b_denoised = self.apply_total_variation_denoising_channel(b, weight, iterations)
        g_denoised = self.apply_total_variation_denoising_channel(g, weight, iterations)
        r_denoised = self.apply_total_variation_denoising_channel(r, weight, iterations)

        # Merge the denoised channels back together
        return cv2.merge([b_denoised, g_denoised, r_denoised])
def main():
    root = tk.Tk()
    app = RunningGaussianAverage(root)
    root.mainloop()
```

```
if __name__ == "__main__":
    main()
```

MOTION DETECTION WITH MIXTURE OF GAUSSIANS (MOG)

DESCRIPTION

The project outlined here introduces a sophisticated application using the Mixture of Gaussians (MOG) method for motion detection, integrated within a Tkinter-based graphical user interface. This application is primarily geared towards users who need to analyze video streams to detect and track motion, leveraging the power of OpenCV's background subtraction capabilities combined with a user-friendly interface.

At its core, the application employs the cv2.createBackgroundSubtractorMOG2(), a method from OpenCV that allows for effective background modeling and foreground detection. This method is known for its ability to handle scenarios with varying lighting conditions and detect shadows, making it highly suitable for security and surveillance purposes. The application initializes this subtractor with specific parameters like history length and variance threshold, which users can adjust to tailor the detection sensitivity to their particular environment.

The GUI layout is meticulously designed to facilitate easy interaction with the video processing functionalities. It features a video display area, playback controls (such as play, pause, stop, and frame navigation), and a mechanism to manually adjust the detection threshold. The integration of list boxes and scrollbars allows users to view and interact with the detection results dynamically, such as observing detected motion areas. This setup not only enhances the usability of the application but also makes it accessible to users with varying levels of technical expertise.

Moreover, the application is equipped with a variety of filtering options to enhance video analysis. Users can apply different filters like Gaussian blur, median blur, or more complex filters such as wavelet transforms and anisotropic diffusion, directly through the GUI. These filters can help in refining the results by reducing noise and improving the clarity of the detected motion areas.

In practice, the application functions by continuously reading frames from a loaded video file, processing each frame to detect motion, and then updating the GUI with the results. This includes drawing bounding boxes around detected regions and listing the coordinates of these regions, providing a clear visual and textual representation of the motion detected within the video. The ability to interactively explore different frames and adjust settings on-the-fly makes it an effective tool for real-time video analysis.

This project exemplifies the integration of advanced image processing techniques within a practical, easy-to-use application, making it an excellent resource for educational purposes, professional security setups, or even for hobbyists interested in video processing technologies. The combination of MOG for motion detection with the flexibility of GUI-driven parameter adjustments and filter applications offers a robust platform for exploring video analytics.

PROCESSING FRAME

```python
def process_frame(self, frame):
    # Convert the frame to grayscale (optional based on approach)
    gray = cv2.cvtColor(frame, cv2.COLOR_BGR2GRAY)
    gray = cv2.GaussianBlur(gray, (21, 21), 0)  # Blur to reduce noise

    # Apply the MOG2 model to get the foreground mask
    fg_mask = self.mog2.apply(gray)

    # Optional: apply additional threshold to clean up the foreground mask
    _, fg_mask = cv2.threshold(fg_mask, self.threshold, 255, cv2.THRESH_BINARY)

    # Find contours on the thresholded image to detect moving objects
    contours, _ = cv2.findContours(fg_mask, cv2.RETR_EXTERNAL, cv2.CHAIN_APPROX_SIMPLE)

    self.listbox.delete(0, tk.END)  # Clear existing entries in the listbox
    box_number = 0  # Initialize box number

    # Loop over the contours
    for contour in contours:
        if cv2.contourArea(contour) < 500:
            continue  # Ignore small contours
        box_number += 1  # Increment the box number for each contour
        (x, y, w, h) = cv2.boundingRect(contour)
        center_x, center_y = x + w // 2, y + h // 2
        cv2.rectangle(frame, (x, y), (x+w, y+h), (50, 0, 255), 2)
        self.listbox.insert(tk.END, f"Box {box_number}: Center ({center_x}, {center_y})")
        cv2.rectangle(frame, (x, y), (x+w, y+h), (50, 0, 255), 2)
        cv2.putText(frame, f"{box_number}", (x + 5, y + 20), cv2.FONT_HERSHEY_SIMPLEX, 0.6, (0, 255, 0), 2)
    self.display_frame(frame)
```

The process_frame() method in the script plays a crucial role in the motion detection application using the Mixture of Gaussians (MOG) approach. Here's a detailed explanation of each step involved in processing a video frame for motion detection:

1. Grayscale Conversion:

    The method starts by converting the input color frame (BGR format) to grayscale using cv2.cvtColor. This simplification step is common in motion detection because it reduces the data complexity by focusing on light intensity, which is sufficient for identifying movement.

2. Noise Reduction:

    After converting to grayscale, the method applies Gaussian Blurring (cv2.GaussianBlur) with a kernel size of (21, 21). This blurring step helps reduce high-frequency noise in the image, which can prevent false detections caused by minor, irrelevant changes in the image.

3. Foreground Mask Generation:

    The preprocessed grayscale image is then fed into an MOG2 background subtractor (self.mog2.apply). This subtractor uses a Gaussian Mixture Model to estimate the background of the video. The frame's pixels that do not fit the background model are considered foreground or moving objects, and a foreground mask is produced.

4. Threshold Application:

    To refine the foreground mask, a binary threshold is applied using cv2.threshold. This operation converts the mask to a binary image where the foreground (detected motion) is marked with white (255) and the background is black (0). The thresholding helps eliminate shadows and other light variations that the MOG2 model might detect as foreground.

5. Contour Detection:

    The method uses cv2.findContours on the thresholded foreground mask to find contours, which are the boundaries of the moving objects detected in the frame.

Contours are useful for further analysis, such as calculating the size and position of the moving objects.

6. Listbox Update and Bounding Box Drawing:

   The application clears previous entries in the listbox (self.listbox.delete(0, tk.END)) to prepare for new motion data. It then loops through each detected contour:

   - It filters out contours smaller than 500 pixels to ignore insignificant movements.
   - For each significant contour, the method calculates its bounding rectangle (cv2.boundingRect), which provides the coordinates and size of the rectangle that encloses the contour.
   - The center of each bounding box is calculated and displayed, along with a rectangle drawn on the original frame to visually indicate the detected movement.
   - Each significant movement's details are added to the listbox and annotated on the frame for visual reference.

7. Frame Display:

   Finally, the modified frame, now annotated with bounding boxes and labels indicating detected motions, is displayed on the GUI's canvas (self.display_frame(frame)). This allows users to see the processed results in real time.

This method effectively integrates various image processing techniques to detect and visualize motion in video frames. It combines the MOG2 background subtraction with additional image manipulation techniques to enhance detection accuracy and user interaction via the graphical interface. Such capabilities make it an excellent tool for applications requiring surveillance, activity monitoring, or any scenario where detecting movement is crucial.

RUNNING PROGRAM

Run program and click on Play/Pause button. Or, you can choose certain frame by pushing Next Frame button. Then, draw a bounding box rectangle on certain object in the frame and push Next Frame button.

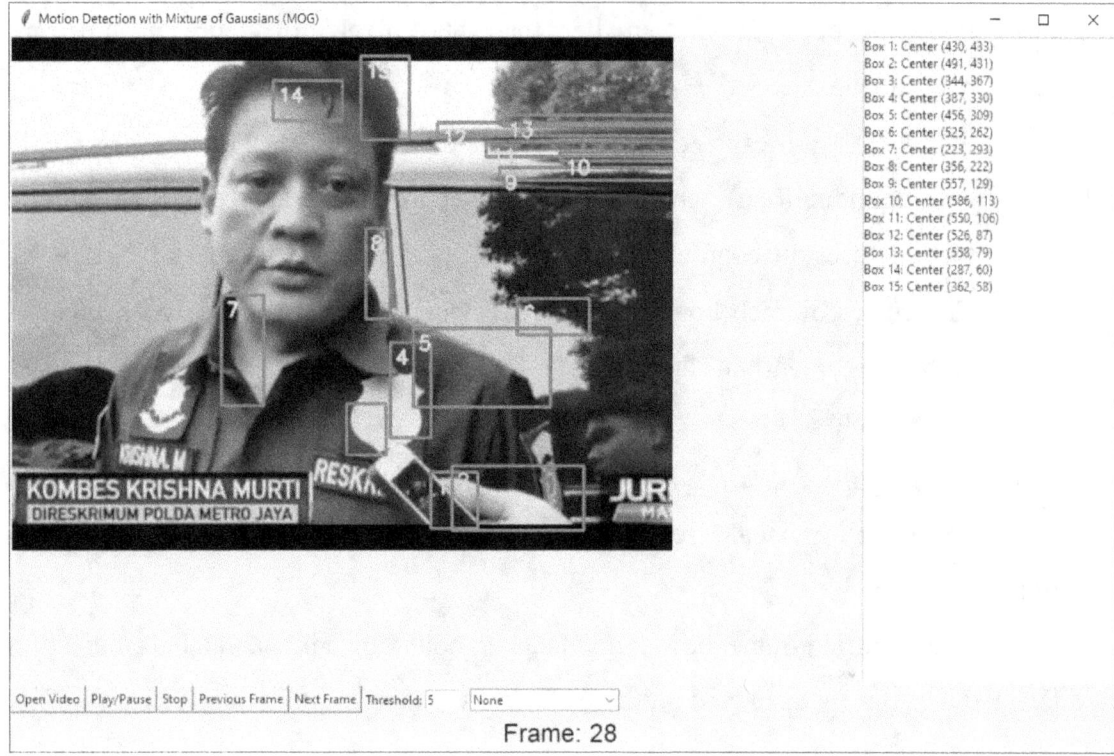

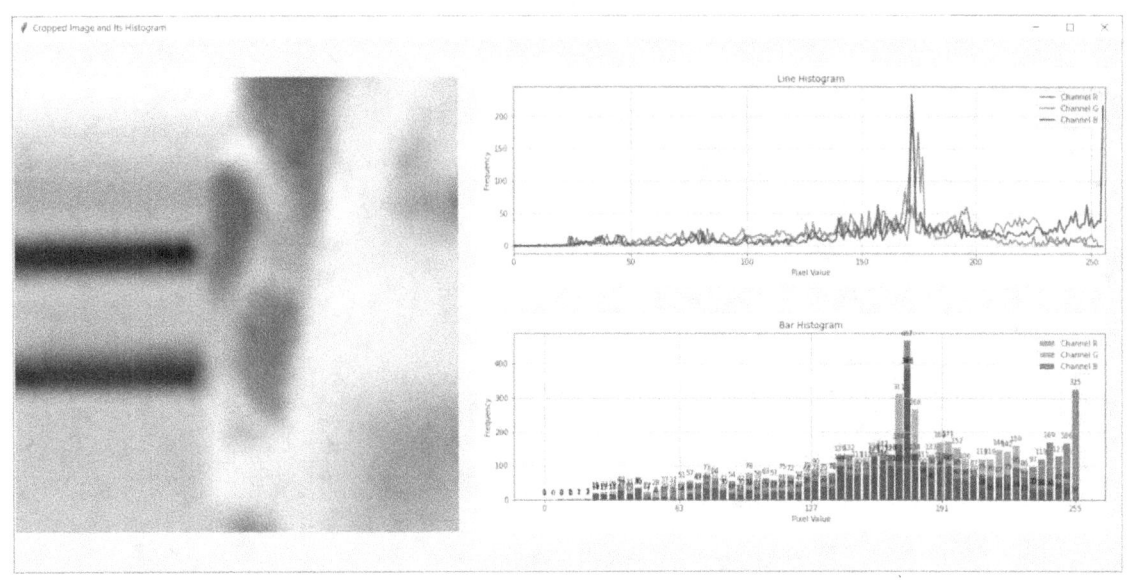

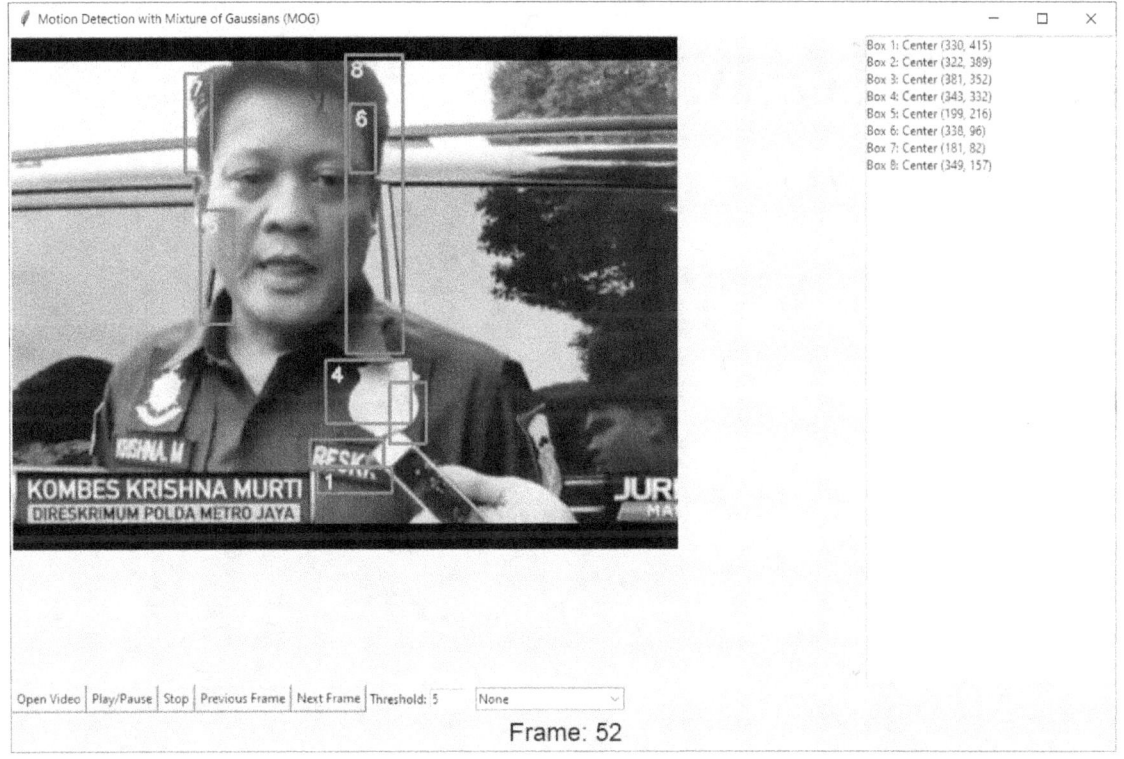

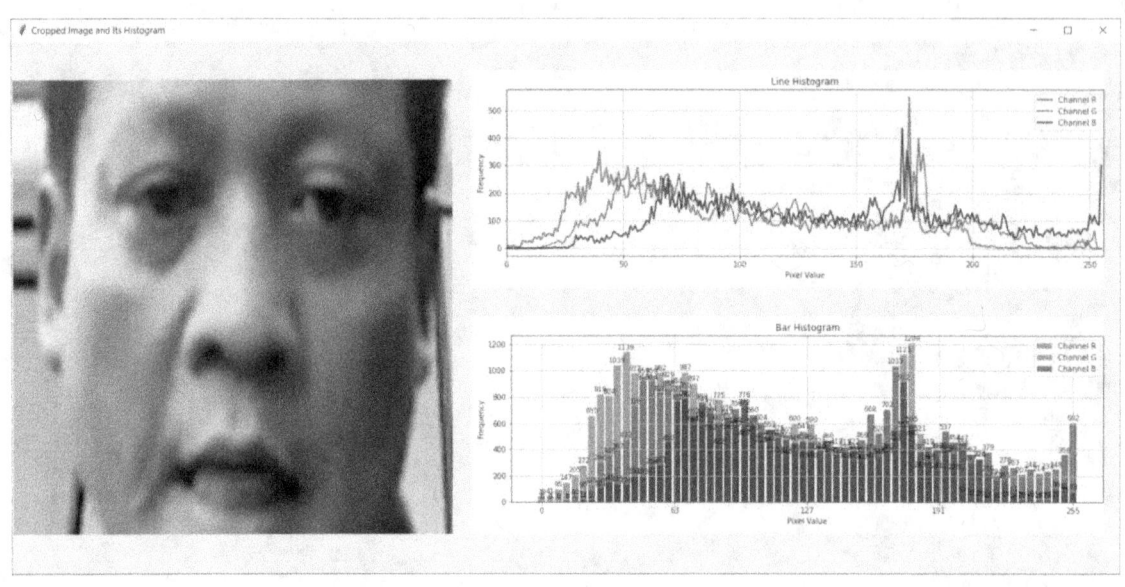

SOURCE CODE

```
#mixture_of_gaussian_with_filtering.py
import tkinter as tk
from tkinter import ttk
from tkinter import filedialog
from PIL import Image, ImageTk
import cv2
import imageio
import matplotlib.pyplot as plt
import pywt
import numpy as np

class MixtureofGaussiansWithFilter:
    def __init__(self, master):
        self.master = master
        self.master.title("Motion Detection with Mixture of Gaussians (MOG)")
        self.bbox_rect = None  # Initialize bbox_rect attribute to None

        # Initialize the MOG2 background subtractor
        self.mog2 = cv2.createBackgroundSubtractorMOG2(history=500, varThreshold=25, detectShadows=True)

        # Video related variables
        self.video = None
```

```python
        self.previous_frame = None
        self.frame_index = 0
        self.paused = True
        self.threshold = 5  # Default threshold for frame differencing

        # Creates widgets
        self.create_widgets(master)

    def create_widgets(self, master):
        # Create a frame for the canvas and listbox
        display_frame = tk.Frame(master)
        display_frame.pack(fill=tk.BOTH, expand=True)

        # Set up the canvas
        self.canvas = tk.Canvas(display_frame, width=800, height=600)
        self.canvas.pack(side=tk.LEFT, fill=tk.BOTH, expand=True)
        self.canvas.bind("<MouseWheel>", self.on_mousewheel)
        self.canvas.bind("<ButtonPress-1>", self.on_press)
        self.canvas.bind("<B1-Motion>", self.on_drag)
        self.canvas.bind("<ButtonRelease-1>", self.on_release)  # Bind ButtonRelease event

        # Set up the listbox for displaying centers
        self.listbox = tk.Listbox(display_frame, width=40, height=20)
        self.listbox.pack(side=tk.RIGHT, fill=tk.Y)

        # Add scrollbar to the listbox
        scrollbar = tk.Scrollbar(display_frame, orient="vertical", command=self.listbox.yview)
        scrollbar.pack(side=tk.RIGHT, fill=tk.Y)
        self.listbox.config(yscrollcommand=scrollbar.set)

        # Control Panel below the display frame
        control_panel = tk.Frame(master)
        control_panel.pack(fill=tk.X)

        self.open_button = tk.Button(control_panel, text="Open Video", command=self.open_video)
        self.open_button.pack(side=tk.LEFT)

        self.play_button = tk.Button(control_panel, text="Play/Pause", command=self.toggle_play_pause)
        self.play_button.pack(side=tk.LEFT)

        self.stop_button = tk.Button(control_panel, text="Stop", command=self.stop_video)
        self.stop_button.pack(side=tk.LEFT)
```

```python
        self.prev_button = tk.Button(control_panel, text="Previous Frame", command=self.prev_frame)
        self.prev_button.pack(side=tk.LEFT)

        self.next_button = tk.Button(control_panel, text="Next Frame", command=self.next_frame)
        self.next_button.pack(side=tk.LEFT)

        # Frame number label
        self.frame_label = tk.Label(master, text="Frame: 0", font=('Helvetica', 18))
        self.frame_label.pack()

        # Threshold Control
        self.threshold_label = tk.Label(control_panel, text="Threshold:")
        self.threshold_label.pack(side=tk.LEFT)

        self.threshold_entry = tk.Entry(control_panel, width=5)
        self.threshold_entry.pack(side=tk.LEFT)
        self.threshold_entry.insert(0, '5')  # Default threshold value
        self.threshold_entry.bind("<Return>", self.update_threshold)

        # Available filters
        self.filters = ["None", "Gaussian", "Mean", "Median", "Bilateral Filtering",
                        "Non-local Means Denoising", "Anisotropic Diffusion",
                        "Total Variation Denoising", "Wiener Filter",
                        "Adaptive Thresholding", "Haar Wavelet Transform",
                        "Daubechies Wavelet Transform"]

        # Subframe for complex controls such as combobox
        filter_frame = tk.Frame(control_panel)
        filter_frame.pack(side=tk.LEFT, fill=tk.X, expand=True)

        # Combobox for Selecting Filters
        self.filter_combobox = ttk.Combobox(filter_frame, values=self.filters)
        self.filter_combobox.pack(side=tk.LEFT, padx=10, pady=5)
        self.filter_combobox.current(0)  # Set default value

    def update_threshold(self, event):
        try:
            self.threshold = int(self.threshold_entry.get())
            print(f"Threshold updated to {self.threshold}")
        except ValueError:
            print("Invalid input for threshold. Please enter an integer.")

    def open_video(self):
        video_path = filedialog.askopenfilename(filetypes=[("Video files", "*.mp4;*.avi;*.mkv;*.wmv")])
        if video_path:
```

```python
            self.video = imageio.get_reader(video_path)
            self.frame_index = 0
            self.previous_frame = None
            self.paused = False
            self.play_video()
            self.update_frame_label()

    def toggle_play_pause(self):
        self.paused = not self.paused
        if not self.paused:
            self.play_video()

    def stop_video(self):
        self.paused = True
        self.frame_index = 0
        self.previous_frame = None
        self.update_frame_label()
        self.display_frame(None)  # Clear the canvas

    def play_video(self):
        if not self.paused and self.video:
            if self.frame_index < len(self.video):
                try:
                    frame_data = self.video.get_data(self.frame_index)
                    frame = cv2.cvtColor(frame_data, cv2.COLOR_RGB2BGR)
                    self.process_frame(frame)
                    self.frame_index += 1
                    self.master.after(42, self.play_video)  # Schedule next frame
                except IndexError:
                    print("Reached the end of the video.")
                    self.paused = True  # Stop the video playback
                self.update_frame_label()

    def process_frame(self, frame):
        # Convert the frame to grayscale (optional based on approach)
        gray = cv2.cvtColor(frame, cv2.COLOR_BGR2GRAY)
        gray = cv2.GaussianBlur(gray, (21, 21), 0)  # Blur to reduce noise

        # Apply the MOG2 model to get the foreground mask
        fg_mask = self.mog2.apply(gray)

        # Optional: apply additional threshold to clean up the foreground mask
        _, fg_mask = cv2.threshold(fg_mask, self.threshold, 255, cv2.THRESH_BINARY)

        # Find contours on the thresholded image to detect moving objects
        contours, _ = cv2.findContours(fg_mask, cv2.RETR_EXTERNAL,
cv2.CHAIN_APPROX_SIMPLE)
```

```python
            self.listbox.delete(0, tk.END)  # Clear existing entries in the listbox
            box_number = 0  # Initialize box number

            # Loop over the contours
            for contour in contours:
                if cv2.contourArea(contour) < 500:
                    continue  # Ignore small contours
                box_number += 1  # Increment the box number for each contour
                (x, y, w, h) = cv2.boundingRect(contour)
                center_x, center_y = x + w // 2, y + h // 2
                cv2.rectangle(frame, (x, y), (x+w, y+h), (50, 0, 255), 2)
                self.listbox.insert(tk.END, f"Box {box_number}: Center ({center_x}, {center_y})")
                cv2.rectangle(frame, (x, y), (x+w, y+h), (50, 0, 255), 2)
                cv2.putText(frame, f"{box_number}", (x + 5, y + 20), cv2.FONT_HERSHEY_SIMPLEX, 0.6, (0, 255, 0), 2)
            self.display_frame(frame)

    def display_frame(self, frame):
        if frame is not None:
            image = cv2.cvtColor(frame, cv2.COLOR_BGR2RGB)
            image = Image.fromarray(image)
            photo = ImageTk.PhotoImage(image=image)
            self.canvas.create_image(0, 0, anchor=tk.NW, image=photo)
            self.canvas.image = photo  # Keep the reference
        else:
            self.canvas.delete("all")

    def process_and_display_frame(self):
        if self.video and self.frame_index >= 0 and self.frame_index < len(self.video):
            try:
                frame_data = self.video.get_data(self.frame_index)
                frame = cv2.cvtColor(frame_data, cv2.COLOR_RGB2BGR)
                self.process_frame(frame)
            except IndexError:
                print(f"Frame index {self.frame_index} is out of range.")
                self.paused = True  # Pause to prevent further errors
            except Exception as e:
                print(f"Error processing frame: {e}")
                self.paused = True
            self.update_frame_label()

    def next_frame(self):
        if self.video and self.frame_index < len(self.video) - 1:  # Check if next frame exists
            self.frame_index += 1
            self.process_and_display_frame()
```

```python
        else:
            print("No more frames to display.")
            self.paused = True

    def prev_frame(self):
        if self.video and self.frame_index > 0:
            self.frame_index -= 1
            self.process_and_display_frame()
        else:
            print("Already at the first frame.")
            self.paused = True


    def update_frame_label(self):
        self.frame_label.config(text=f"Frame: {self.frame_index}")

    def on_mousewheel(self, event):
        direction = event.delta // 120
        current_value = int(self.zoom_scale.get())
        if direction == 1 and current_value < 10:
            current_value += 1
        elif direction == -1 and current_value > 1:
            current_value -= 1
        self.zoom_scale.set(current_value)
        self.update_zoom()

    def on_press(self, event):
        self.tracker = None
        self.start_x = self.canvas.canvasx(event.x)
        self.start_y = self.canvas.canvasy(event.y)
        # Clear the previous bounding box if it exists
        if self.bbox_rect:
            self.canvas.delete(self.bbox_rect)
            self.bbox_rect = None
        self.bbox = None
        self.bbox2 = None

    def on_drag(self, event):
        # Update the endpoint of the rectangle as the mouse moves
        cur_x = self.canvas.canvasx(event.x)
        cur_y = self.canvas.canvasy(event.y)

        # Define the coordinates correctly ensuring x1 < x2 and y1 < y2
        x1, y1 = min(self.start_x, cur_x), min(self.start_y, cur_y)
        x2, y2 = max(self.start_x, cur_x), max(self.start_y, cur_y)

        # Update dimensions for tracking
        self.initial_w = x2 - x1
```

```python
        self.initial_h = y2 - y1
        self.bbox = (x1, y1, self.initial_w, self.initial_h)
        self.bbox2 = (self.start_x, self.start_y, cur_x, cur_y)

        # Update or create a rectangle on the canvas
        if self.bbox_rect:
            self.canvas.coords(self.bbox_rect, x1, y1, x2, y2)
        else:
            self.bbox_rect = self.canvas.create_rectangle(x1, y1, x2, y2, outline="cyan", width=6)

    def on_release(self, event):
        self.analyze_histogram()  # Call analyze_histogram() method when the mouse button is released

    def analyze_histogram(self):
        if self.bbox2 is not None and self.video:
            x1, y1, x2, y2 = map(int, self.bbox2)
            if x1 != x2 and y1 != y2:
                try:
                    frame = self.video.get_data(self.frame_index)
                    # Ensure the bounding box is within the frame boundaries
                    h, w, _ = frame.shape
                    x1, x2 = max(0, min(x1, w)), max(0, min(x2, w))
                    y1, y2 = max(0, min(y1, h)), max(0, min(y2, h))

                    # Ensure x1 < x2 and y1 < y2
                    x1, x2 = sorted([x1, x2])
                    y1, y2 = sorted([y1, y2])

                    cropped_frame = frame[y1:y2, x1:x2]
                    if cropped_frame.size > 0:
                        cropped_frame = cv2.cvtColor(cropped_frame, cv2.COLOR_BGR2RGB)

                        # Get selected filter from combobox
                        selected_filter = self.filter_combobox.get()
                        # Apply selected filter
                        filtered_frame = self.apply_filter(selected_filter, cropped_frame)

                        self.create_popup_window(filtered_frame)
                        self.display_cropped_image(filtered_frame)
                        self.display_histograms(filtered_frame)
                    else:
                        print("Cropped frame is empty.")
                except Exception as e:
                    print("Failed to process frame:", e)
```

```python
        else:
            print("Bounding box dimensions are zero or negative.")


def create_popup_window(self, cropped_frame):
    self.popup_window = tk.Toplevel(self.master)
    self.popup_window.title("Cropped Image and Its Histogram")
    self.popup_window.geometry("1500x700")


def display_cropped_image(self, cropped_frame):
    cropped_frame_frame = tk.Frame(self.popup_window)
    cropped_frame_frame.pack(side="left")

    cropped_frame_rgb = cv2.cvtColor(cropped_frame, cv2.COLOR_BGR2RGB)
    cropped_img = Image.fromarray(cropped_frame_rgb)
    cropped_img = cropped_img.resize((600, 600))

    cropped_photo = ImageTk.PhotoImage(cropped_img)
    cropped_canvas = tk.Canvas(cropped_frame_frame, width=600, height=600)
    cropped_canvas.pack(side="left", anchor="nw")
    cropped_canvas.create_image(0, 0, anchor="nw", image=cropped_photo)
    cropped_canvas.image = cropped_photo

def display_histograms(self, cropped_frame):
    histograms_frame = tk.Frame(self.popup_window)
    histograms_frame.pack(side="right", padx=20)

    self.display_line_histogram(cropped_frame, histograms_frame)
    self.display_bar_histogram(cropped_frame, histograms_frame)

def display_line_histogram(self, cropped_frame, histograms_frame):
    line_histogram_frame = tk.Frame(histograms_frame)
    line_histogram_frame.pack(side="top", pady=10)

    plt.figure(figsize=(12, 4))
    color = ('r', 'g', 'b')
    for i, col in enumerate(color):
        histr = cv2.calcHist([cropped_frame], [i], None, [256], [0, 256])
        plt.plot(histr, color=col, label=f'Channel {col.upper()}', linewidth=2)
        plt.xlim([0, 256])
    plt.title('Line Histogram')
    plt.xlabel('Pixel Value')
    plt.ylabel('Frequency')
    plt.tight_layout()
    plt.grid(True)
    plt.legend()
```

```python
        line_histogram_img = self.plot_to_image(plt)
        self.display_histogram_image(line_histogram_frame, line_histogram_img)

    def display_bar_histogram(self, cropped_frame, histograms_frame):
        bar_histogram_frame = tk.Frame(histograms_frame)
        bar_histogram_frame.pack(side="bottom", pady=10)

        plt.figure(figsize=(12, 4))
        color = ('r', 'g', 'b')
        for i, col in enumerate(color):
            hist_range = (0, 256)
            hist_counts, _ = np.histogram(cropped_frame[:, :, i], bins=64, range=hist_range)
            plt.bar(np.arange(64), hist_counts, color=col, alpha=0.7, label=f'Channel {col.upper()}')
            for index, value in enumerate(hist_counts):
                plt.text(index, value + 10, str(int(value)), ha='center', va='bottom', fontsize=9)

        plt.title('Bar Histogram')
        plt.xlabel('Pixel Value')
        plt.ylabel('Frequency')
        plt.xticks(np.linspace(0, 63, num=5), np.linspace(0, 255, num=5, dtype=int))  # Adjust x-axis ticks
        plt.tight_layout()
        plt.grid(True)
        plt.legend()

        bar_histogram_img = self.plot_to_image(plt)
        self.display_histogram_image(bar_histogram_frame, bar_histogram_img)

    def display_histogram_image(self, parent_frame, img):
        histogram_photo = ImageTk.PhotoImage(image=img)
        histogram_canvas = tk.Canvas(parent_frame, width=900, height=300)
        histogram_canvas.pack(side="bottom", anchor="se")
        histogram_canvas.create_image(0, 0, anchor="nw", image=histogram_photo)
        histogram_canvas.image = histogram_photo

    def plot_histogram_bar_to_image(self, image):
        # Calculate histogram for each channel
        histograms = []
        for i in range(3):
            hist_range = (0, 256)
            hist_counts, _ = np.histogram(image[:, :, i], bins=64, range=hist_range)  # Adjust bins to 64
            histograms.append(hist_counts)

        # Extracting only 64 bins from the histogram
```

```python
        num_bins = 64  # Adjusted to 64 bins

        # Generating colors for each channel
        colors = ['red', 'green', 'blue']

        plt.figure()
        for i, histogram in enumerate(histograms):
            # Normalize the histogram counts for better visualization
            hist_counts = histogram / np.sum(histogram)
            # Setting the color for each channel
            plt.bar(np.arange(num_bins), hist_counts[:num_bins], color=colors[i], alpha=0.7, label=f'Channel {["Red", "Green", "Blue"][i]}')

        plt.xlabel('Pixel Value')
        plt.ylabel('Normalized Frequency')
        plt.title('RGB Channel Histograms')
        plt.grid(True)
        plt.tight_layout()
        plt.legend()

        # Convert the histogram bar graph to an image
        histogram_bar_img = self.plot_to_image(plt)
        histogram_bar_photo = ImageTk.PhotoImage(image=histogram_bar_img)

        return histogram_bar_photo

    def plot_to_image(self, plt):
        plt.savefig('temp_plot.png')
        img = Image.open('temp_plot.png')
        return img

    def apply_filter(self, filter_name, frame):
        if filter_name == "None":
            return frame
        elif filter_name == "Gaussian":
            return cv2.GaussianBlur(frame, (5, 5), 0)
        elif filter_name == "Mean":
            return cv2.blur(frame, (5, 5))
        elif filter_name == "Median":
            return cv2.medianBlur(frame, 5)
        elif filter_name == "Bilateral Filtering":
            return cv2.bilateralFilter(frame, 9, 75, 75)
        elif filter_name == "Non-local Means Denoising":
            return cv2.fastNlMeansDenoisingColored(frame, None, 10, 10, 7, 21)
        elif filter_name == "Anisotropic Diffusion":
            return self.anisotropic_diffusion(frame)
        elif filter_name == "Total Variation Denoising":
            return self.total_variation_denoising(frame)
```

```python
        elif filter_name == "Wiener Filter":
            return self.wiener_filter(frame)
        elif filter_name == "Adaptive Thresholding":
            return self.adaptive_threshold_each_channel(frame)
        elif filter_name == "Haar Wavelet Transform":
            return self.haar_wavelet_transform(frame)
        elif filter_name == "Daubechies Wavelet Transform":
            return self.daubechies_wavelet_transform(frame)
        else:
            return frame  # Default: return original frame if filter not found

    def wiener_filter(self, frame, kernel_size=(5, 5), noise_var=0.01):
        # Check if frame is None
        if frame is None:
            print("Error: Input frame is None.")
            return None

        # Check if frame is a valid numpy array
        if not isinstance(frame, np.ndarray):
            print("Error: Input frame is not a numpy array.")
            return None

        # Check if frame is an empty array
        if frame.size == 0:
            print("Error: Input frame is empty.")
            return None

        # Check if frame is in BGR color space
        if frame.shape[-1] != 3:
            print("Error: Input frame is not in BGR color space.")
            return None

        # Apply Wiener filter
        filtered_frame = cv2.medianBlur(frame, kernel_size[0])  # Use kernel_size[0] as the kernel size
        filtered_frame = cv2.fastNlMeansDenoising(filtered_frame, h=noise_var)
        return filtered_frame

    def adaptive_threshold_each_channel(self, frame):
        # Split the frame into individual channels
        b, g, r = cv2.split(frame)

        # Apply adaptive thresholding to each channel separately
        b_thresh = cv2.adaptiveThreshold(b, 255, cv2.ADAPTIVE_THRESH_GAUSSIAN_C, cv2.THRESH_BINARY, 11, 2)
        g_thresh = cv2.adaptiveThreshold(g, 255, cv2.ADAPTIVE_THRESH_GAUSSIAN_C, cv2.THRESH_BINARY, 11, 2)
```

```python
            r_thresh = cv2.adaptiveThreshold(r, 255, cv2.ADAPTIVE_THRESH_GAUSSIAN_C,
cv2.THRESH_BINARY, 11, 2)

            # Merge the thresholded channels back together
            return cv2.merge([b_thresh, g_thresh, r_thresh])

    def haar_wavelet_transform(self, frame):
        # Split the frame into its individual color channels
        b, g, r = cv2.split(frame)

        # Perform the wavelet transform on each channel separately
        b_coeffs = pywt.dwt2(b, 'haar')
        g_coeffs = pywt.dwt2(g, 'haar')
        r_coeffs = pywt.dwt2(r, 'haar')

        # Reconstruct the channels from the coefficients
        b_reconstructed = pywt.idwt2(b_coeffs, 'haar')
        g_reconstructed = pywt.idwt2(g_coeffs, 'haar')
        r_reconstructed = pywt.idwt2(r_coeffs, 'haar')

        # Clip the values to ensure they are within the valid range
        b_reconstructed = np.clip(b_reconstructed, 0, 255).astype(np.uint8)
        g_reconstructed = np.clip(g_reconstructed, 0, 255).astype(np.uint8)
        r_reconstructed = np.clip(r_reconstructed, 0, 255).astype(np.uint8)

        # Merge the channels back together
        return cv2.merge([b_reconstructed, g_reconstructed, r_reconstructed])

    def daubechies_wavelet_transform(self, frame):
        # Split the frame into its individual color channels
        b, g, r = cv2.split(frame)

        # Choose the wavelet function (Daubechies 5)
        wavelet = 'db5'

        # Perform the wavelet transform on each channel separately
        b_coeffs = pywt.dwt2(b, wavelet)
        g_coeffs = pywt.dwt2(g, wavelet)
        r_coeffs = pywt.dwt2(r, wavelet)

        # Reconstruct the channels from the coefficients
        b_reconstructed = pywt.idwt2(b_coeffs, wavelet)
        g_reconstructed = pywt.idwt2(g_coeffs, wavelet)
        r_reconstructed = pywt.idwt2(r_coeffs, wavelet)

        # Clip the values to ensure they are within the valid range
        b_reconstructed = np.clip(b_reconstructed, 0, 255).astype(np.uint8)
        g_reconstructed = np.clip(g_reconstructed, 0, 255).astype(np.uint8)
```

```python
            r_reconstructed = np.clip(r_reconstructed, 0, 255).astype(np.uint8)

            # Merge the channels back together
            return cv2.merge([b_reconstructed, g_reconstructed, r_reconstructed])

    def anisotropic_diffusion(self, img):
        return cv2.fastNlMeansDenoisingColored(img, None, 10, 10, 7, 21)

    def apply_total_variation_denoising_channel(self, channel, weight, iterations):
        # Initialize the result with the original channel
        result = channel.copy().astype(np.float64)  # Convert to float64

        # Perform total variation denoising
        for _ in range(iterations):
            # Compute the gradient of the channel
            dx = cv2.Sobel(result, cv2.CV_64F, 1, 0, ksize=3)
            dy = cv2.Sobel(result, cv2.CV_64F, 0, 1, ksize=3)

            # Update the channel using the gradient and the weight
            result -= weight * np.sqrt(dx**2 + dy**2)

        # Clip the values to ensure they are within the valid range
        result = np.clip(result, 0, 255).astype(np.uint8)

        return result

    def total_variation_denoising(self, img, weight=0.01, iterations=20):
        # Split the image into its individual color channels
        b, g, r = cv2.split(img)

        # Apply total variation denoising to each channel separately
        b_denoised = self.apply_total_variation_denoising_channel(b, weight, iterations)
        g_denoised = self.apply_total_variation_denoising_channel(g, weight, iterations)
        r_denoised = self.apply_total_variation_denoising_channel(r, weight, iterations)

        # Merge the denoised channels back together
        return cv2.merge([b_denoised, g_denoised, r_denoised])
def main():
    root = tk.Tk()
    app = MixtureofGaussiansWithFilter(root)
    root.mainloop()

if __name__ == "__main__":
    main()
```

MOTION DETECTION WITH KERNEL DENSITY ESTIMATION

DESCRIPTION

The script outlines the development of a sophisticated motion detection system employing Kernel Density Estimation (KDE) for analyzing video data, integrated into a user-friendly graphical interface using Tkinter. This project, named "Motion Detection with Kernel Density Estimation," leverages advanced image processing techniques encapsulated in a GUI to enhance usability and accessibility for users who may not be experts in programming or image processing.

At the core of this application is the initialization of the MOG2 background subtractor, a method from the OpenCV library designed to differentiate between the background and foreground elements in video streams. This subtractor is particularly effective in environments with variable lighting and can detect shadows, making it highly suitable for robust motion detection in diverse settings. The application not only initializes this subtractor but also sets up a motion density map to accumulate motion data over time, providing a comprehensive view of movement patterns across frames.

The user interface is designed for ease of use, featuring a main display area where video frames are rendered, alongside controls for video playback including play, pause, stop, and navigation through video frames. This allows users to interactively manage the video feed and directly observe the effects of their adjustments on the motion detection output. Additionally, the interface includes a listbox for displaying detected motion events and a set of filters that users can apply to enhance or alter the video feed, such as Gaussian blur or wavelet transforms.

In operation, the system processes each frame by converting it to grayscale and applying a Gaussian blur to reduce noise, which helps in enhancing the accuracy of the motion detection algorithm. Following this preprocessing, the MOG2 model calculates a foreground mask, which is then refined using a binary threshold to clearly delineate areas of motion. This mask updates a motion density map that accumulates motion data, providing a richer context for detecting persistent or significant movements.

Contour detection techniques are employed on the thresholded mask to identify distinct areas of motion, with each identified contour potentially corresponding to a moving object. These are visually marked on the video feed, and details such as the center and boundary of each movement are displayed on the interface. This not only helps in monitoring and recording motion events but also enhances the analytical capabilities of the system by allowing users to see a detailed breakdown of all movements within the video.

Overall, this project integrates complex image processing tasks into a practical application, making powerful motion detection technologies accessible and usable for a broad audience. It exemplifies how advanced computational methods can be effectively combined with user-friendly interfaces to create tools that are both powerful and easy to use, catering to needs in surveillance, research, and other fields where motion detection is applicable.

PROCESSING FRAME

```python
def process_frame(self, frame):
    gray = cv2.cvtColor(frame, cv2.COLOR_BGR2GRAY)
    gray = cv2.GaussianBlur(gray, (21, 21), 0)

    # Apply the MOG2 model to get the foreground mask
    fg_mask = self.mog2.apply(gray)
    _, fg_mask = cv2.threshold(fg_mask, self.threshold, 255, cv2.THRESH_BINARY)

    # Update the motion density map
    if self.motion_density is None:
        self.motion_density = np.zeros_like(gray, dtype=float)
    # Accumulate the motion information
    self.motion_density += fg_mask.astype(float)

    # Optionally apply Gaussian blur to simulate KDE smoothing
    density_smoothed = cv2.GaussianBlur(self.motion_density, (21, 21), 0)
    density_normalized = np.clip((density_smoothed / density_smoothed.max()) * 255, 0, 255).astype(np.uint8)

    # Find contours on the thresholded image to detect moving objects
    contours, _ = cv2.findContours(fg_mask, cv2.RETR_EXTERNAL, cv2.CHAIN_APPROX_SIMPLE)

    self.listbox.delete(0, tk.END)
    box_number = 0

    # First, display the density map to set it as background
    background_image = cv2.applyColorMap(density_normalized, cv2.COLORMAP_JET)

    for contour in contours:
        if cv2.contourArea(contour) < 500:
            continue
        box_number += 1
        (x, y, w, h) = cv2.boundingRect(contour)
```

```
            center_x, center_y = x + w // 2, y + h // 2

            # Draw rectangle and text over the background image
            cv2.rectangle(background_image, (x, y), (x+w, y+h), (255, 255, 255), 2)
            cv2.putText(background_image, f"{box_number}", (x + 5, y + 20),
cv2.FONT_HERSHEY_SIMPLEX, 0.6, (0, 0, 0), 2)
            self.listbox.insert(tk.END, f"Box {box_number}: Center ({center_x},
{center_y})")

        # Display the final image (density map + bounding boxes)
        self.display_frame(background_image)
```

The process_frame() method in your script is a sophisticated function designed to process video frames for motion detection using Kernel Density Estimation (KDE) techniques combined with background subtraction via MOG2. The method effectively highlights areas of motion and visually represents this data using a color-mapped density map. Here's a detailed breakdown of how each step in the method contributes to detecting and visualizing motion in video frames:

1. Grayscale Conversion:

    The first step involves converting the RGB frame to grayscale using cv2.cvtColor. This conversion simplifies the image data, reducing the computational complexity required for subsequent processing steps.

2. Noise Reduction:

    The grayscale image is then blurred using a Gaussian Blur (cv2.GaussianBlur with a kernel size of (21, 21)). This blurring helps to reduce noise and smooth out the image, which is crucial for improving the accuracy of motion detection by minimizing false positives caused by minor fluctuations in pixel values.

3. Foreground Mask Creation:

    The MOG2 background subtraction method (self.mog2.apply) is applied to the blurred image to generate a foreground mask. This mask distinguishes moving objects from the static background. The mask is further refined through thresholding (cv2.threshold), where the pixel intensity is set to maximum where the foreground is detected, effectively isolating areas of movement.

4. Motion Density Map Update:
   - If the motion density map is uninitialized (self.motion_density is None), it is created as a floating-point zero matrix of the same dimensions as the grayscale frame. This map accumulates values from the thresholded foreground mask over time, thus building up a picture of where motion occurs most frequently in the video.
   - The foreground mask is added to this density map (self.motion_density += fg_mask.astype(float)), and Gaussian blurring is optionally applied again to simulate the smoothing effect characteristic of KDE, which helps in visualizing the spread and intensity of motion across frames.
5. Contour Detection:

   Contours are detected from the thresholded foreground mask (cv2.findContours). These contours outline the individual moving objects or areas of significant motion in the frame.
6. Visualization:
   - A background image for display is created by applying a color map (cv2.applyColorMap) to the normalized motion density map. This color-mapped image serves as a visual representation of motion intensity and distribution, with warmer colors typically indicating areas of higher motion density.
   - Each detected contour is processed to calculate bounding boxes (cv2.boundingRect), which are drawn onto the color-mapped background along with labels indicating the sequence of the detected motion (box numbers).
   - Information about each significant motion detected (such as the center of the bounding box) is added to a listbox in the GUI, which provides a textual overview of the motion events.
7. Frame Display:

Finally, the color-mapped image with annotated motion data is displayed on the application's canvas. This visual output allows users to see both the density and specific locations of motion in a comprehensive and intuitive manner.

This method cleverly combines analytical techniques with practical visualization tools, making it highly effective for applications where understanding spatial and temporal patterns of movement is crucial, such as in surveillance, human-computer interaction studies, or environmental monitoring.

RUNNING PROGRAM

Run program and click on Play/Pause button. Or, you can choose certain frame by pushing Next Frame button. Then, draw a bounding box rectangle on certain object in the frame and push Next Frame button.

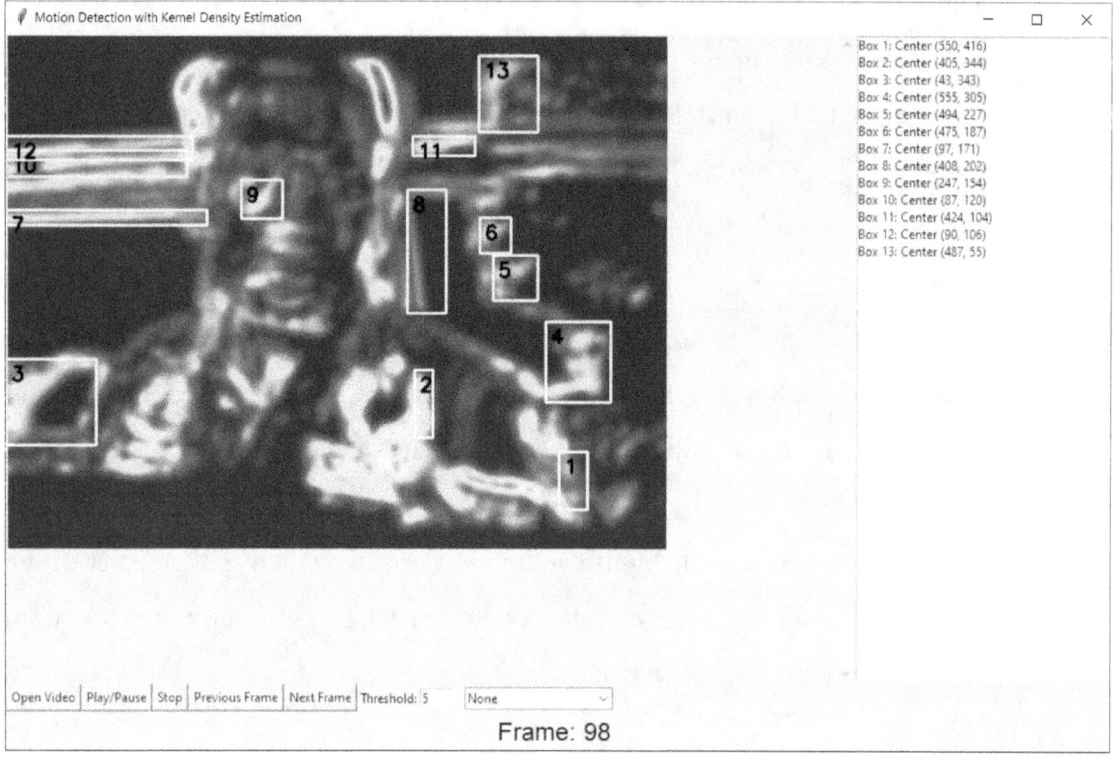

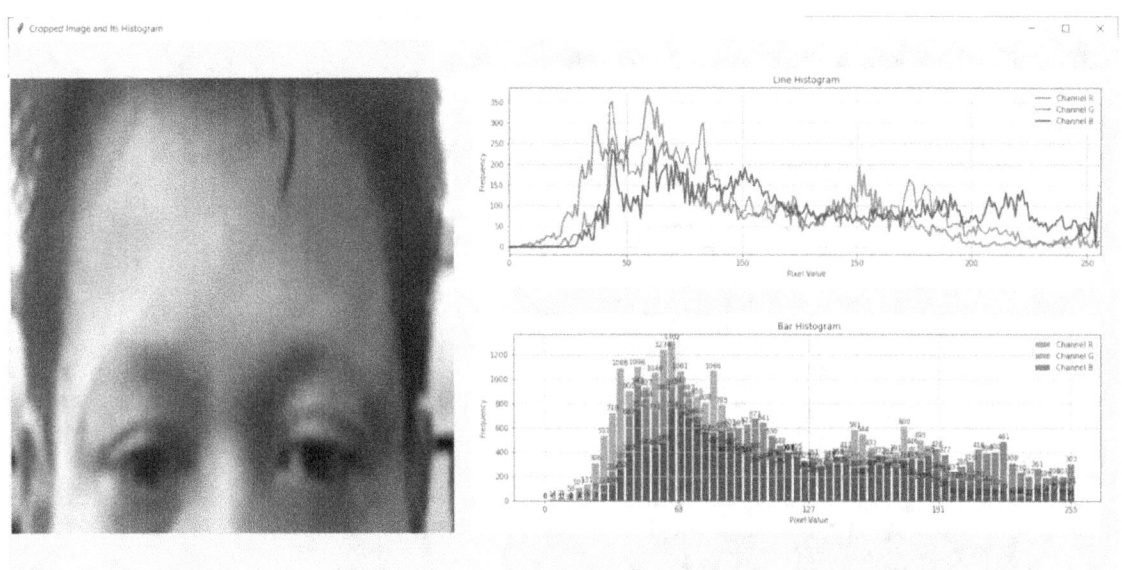

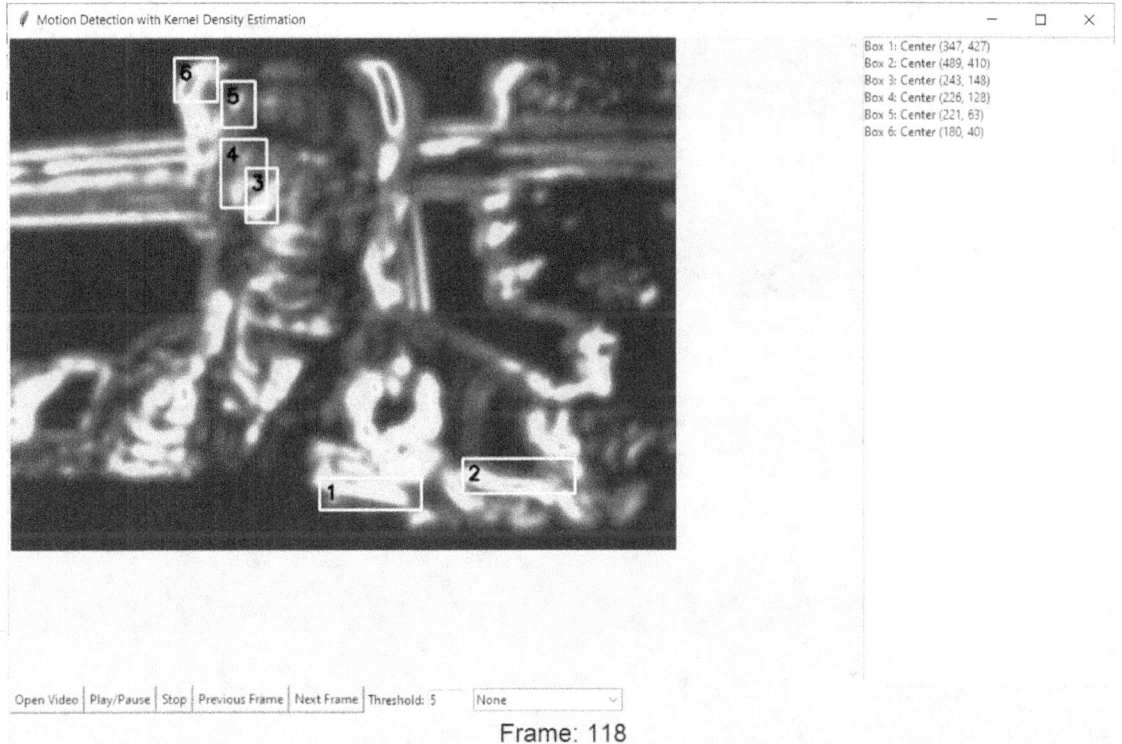

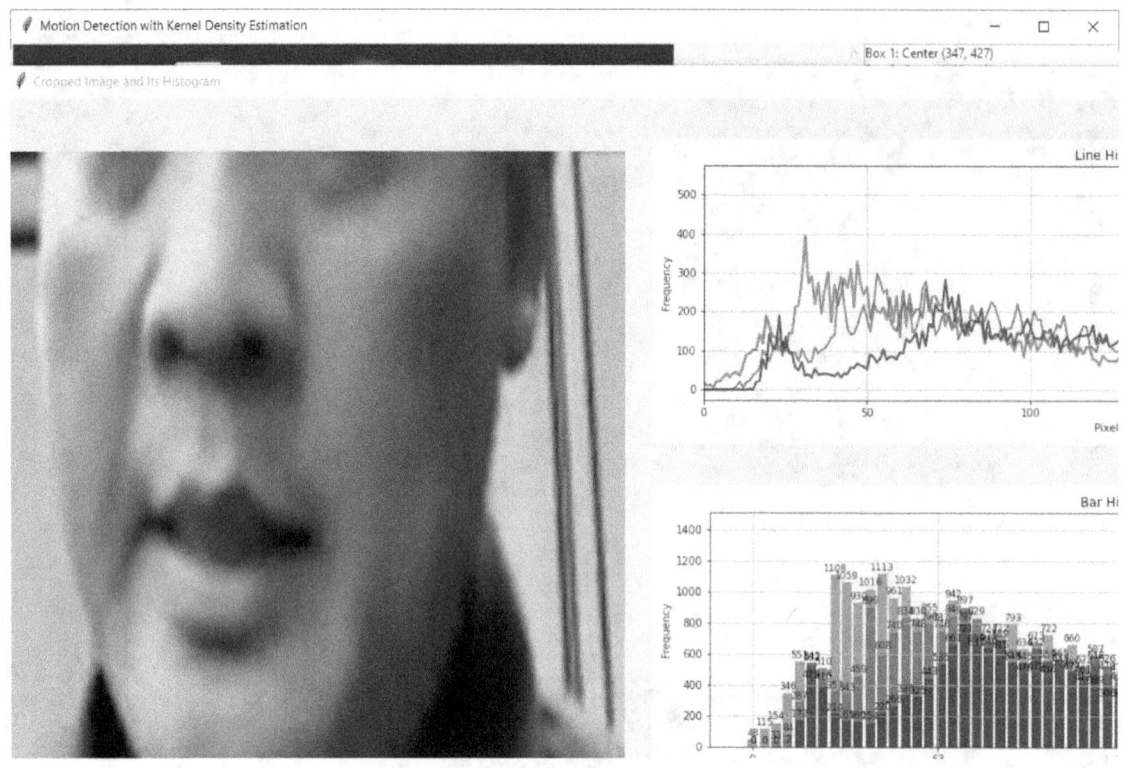

SOURCE CODE

```
#kernel_density_estimation_with_filtering.py
import tkinter as tk
from tkinter import ttk
from tkinter import filedialog
from PIL import Image, ImageTk
import cv2
import imageio
import matplotlib.pyplot as plt
import pywt
import numpy as np

class KDEWithFilter:
    def __init__(self, master):
        self.master = master
        self.master.title("Motion Detection with Kernel Density Estimation")
        self.bbox_rect = None  # Initialize bbox_rect attribute to None
```

```python
        # Initialize the MOG2 background subtractor
        self.mog2 = cv2.createBackgroundSubtractorMOG2(history=500, varThreshold=25, detectShadows=True)
        self.motion_density = None  # Initialize the motion density map

        # Video related variables
        self.video = None
        self.previous_frame = None
        self.frame_index = 0
        self.paused = True
        self.threshold = 5  # Default threshold for frame differencing

        # Creates widgets
        self.create_widgets(master)

    def create_widgets(self, master):
        # Create a frame for the canvas and listbox
        display_frame = tk.Frame(master)
        display_frame.pack(fill=tk.BOTH, expand=True)

        # Set up the canvas
        self.canvas = tk.Canvas(display_frame, width=800, height=600)
        self.canvas.pack(side=tk.LEFT, fill=tk.BOTH, expand=True)
        self.canvas.bind("<MouseWheel>", self.on_mousewheel)
        self.canvas.bind("<ButtonPress-1>", self.on_press)
        self.canvas.bind("<B1-Motion>", self.on_drag)
        self.canvas.bind("<ButtonRelease-1>", self.on_release)  # Bind ButtonRelease event

        # Set up the listbox for displaying centers
        self.listbox = tk.Listbox(display_frame, width=40, height=20)
        self.listbox.pack(side=tk.RIGHT, fill=tk.Y)

        # Add scrollbar to the listbox
        scrollbar = tk.Scrollbar(display_frame, orient="vertical", command=self.listbox.yview)
        scrollbar.pack(side=tk.RIGHT, fill=tk.Y)
        self.listbox.config(yscrollcommand=scrollbar.set)

        # Control Panel below the display frame
        control_panel = tk.Frame(master)
        control_panel.pack(fill=tk.X)

        self.open_button = tk.Button(control_panel, text="Open Video", command=self.open_video)
        self.open_button.pack(side=tk.LEFT)
```

```python
        self.play_button = tk.Button(control_panel, text="Play/Pause", 
command=self.toggle_play_pause)
        self.play_button.pack(side=tk.LEFT)
        
        self.stop_button = tk.Button(control_panel, text="Stop", 
command=self.stop_video)
        self.stop_button.pack(side=tk.LEFT)
        
        self.prev_button = tk.Button(control_panel, text="Previous Frame", 
command=self.prev_frame)
        self.prev_button.pack(side=tk.LEFT)
        
        self.next_button = tk.Button(control_panel, text="Next Frame", 
command=self.next_frame)
        self.next_button.pack(side=tk.LEFT)
        
        # Frame number label
        self.frame_label = tk.Label(master, text="Frame: 0", font=('Helvetica', 18))
        self.frame_label.pack()
        
        # Threshold Control
        self.threshold_label = tk.Label(control_panel, text="Threshold:")
        self.threshold_label.pack(side=tk.LEFT)
        
        self.threshold_entry = tk.Entry(control_panel, width=5)
        self.threshold_entry.pack(side=tk.LEFT)
        self.threshold_entry.insert(0, '5')  # Default threshold value
        self.threshold_entry.bind("<Return>", self.update_threshold)
        
        # Available filters
        self.filters = ["None", "Gaussian", "Mean", "Median", "Bilateral Filtering",
                       "Non-local Means Denoising", "Anisotropic Diffusion",
                       "Total Variation Denoising", "Wiener Filter",
                       "Adaptive Thresholding", "Haar Wavelet Transform",
                       "Daubechies Wavelet Transform"]
        
        # Subframe for complex controls such as combobox
        filter_frame = tk.Frame(control_panel)
        filter_frame.pack(side=tk.LEFT, fill=tk.X, expand=True)
        
        # Combobox for Selecting Filters
        self.filter_combobox = ttk.Combobox(filter_frame, values=self.filters)
        self.filter_combobox.pack(side=tk.LEFT, padx=10, pady=5)
        self.filter_combobox.current(0)  # Set default value
        
    def update_threshold(self, event):
        try:
            self.threshold = int(self.threshold_entry.get())
```

```python
                print(f"Threshold updated to {self.threshold}")
        except ValueError:
            print("Invalid input for threshold. Please enter an integer.")

    def open_video(self):
        video_path = filedialog.askopenfilename(filetypes=[("Video files", 
"*.mp4;*.avi;*.mkv;*.wmv")])
        if video_path:
            self.video = imageio.get_reader(video_path)
            self.frame_index = 0
            self.previous_frame = None
            self.paused = False
            self.play_video()
            self.update_frame_label()

    def toggle_play_pause(self):
        self.paused = not self.paused
        if not self.paused:
            self.play_video()

    def stop_video(self):
        self.paused = True
        self.frame_index = 0
        self.previous_frame = None
        self.update_frame_label()
        self.display_frame(None)  # Clear the canvas

    def play_video(self):
        if not self.paused and self.video:
            if self.frame_index < len(self.video):
                try:
                    frame_data = self.video.get_data(self.frame_index)
                    frame = cv2.cvtColor(frame_data, cv2.COLOR_RGB2BGR)
                    self.process_frame(frame)
                    self.frame_index += 1
                    self.master.after(42, self.play_video)  # Schedule next frame
                except IndexError:
                    print("Reached the end of the video.")
                    self.paused = True  # Stop the video playback
                self.update_frame_label()

    def process_frame(self, frame):
        gray = cv2.cvtColor(frame, cv2.COLOR_BGR2GRAY)
        gray = cv2.GaussianBlur(gray, (21, 21), 0)

        # Apply the MOG2 model to get the foreground mask
        fg_mask = self.mog2.apply(gray)
        _, fg_mask = cv2.threshold(fg_mask, self.threshold, 255, cv2.THRESH_BINARY)
```

```python
        # Update the motion density map
        if self.motion_density is None:
            self.motion_density = np.zeros_like(gray, dtype=float)
        # Accumulate the motion information
        self.motion_density += fg_mask.astype(float)

        # Optionally apply Gaussian blur to simulate KDE smoothing
        density_smoothed = cv2.GaussianBlur(self.motion_density, (21, 21), 0)
        density_normalized = np.clip((density_smoothed / density_smoothed.max()) * 255, 0, 255).astype(np.uint8)

        # Find contours on the thresholded image to detect moving objects
        contours, _ = cv2.findContours(fg_mask, cv2.RETR_EXTERNAL, cv2.CHAIN_APPROX_SIMPLE)

        self.listbox.delete(0, tk.END)
        box_number = 0

        # First, display the density map to set it as background
        background_image = cv2.applyColorMap(density_normalized, cv2.COLORMAP_JET)

        for contour in contours:
            if cv2.contourArea(contour) < 500:
                continue
            box_number += 1
            (x, y, w, h) = cv2.boundingRect(contour)
            center_x, center_y = x + w // 2, y + h // 2

            # Draw rectangle and text over the background image
            cv2.rectangle(background_image, (x, y), (x+w, y+h), (255, 255, 255), 2)
            cv2.putText(background_image, f"{box_number}", (x + 5, y + 20), cv2.FONT_HERSHEY_SIMPLEX, 0.6, (0, 0, 0), 2)
            self.listbox.insert(tk.END, f"Box {box_number}: Center ({center_x}, {center_y})")

        # Display the final image (density map + bounding boxes)
        self.display_frame(background_image)

    def display_frame(self, frame):
        if frame is not None:
            image = cv2.cvtColor(frame, cv2.COLOR_BGR2RGB)
            image = Image.fromarray(image)
            photo = ImageTk.PhotoImage(image=image)
            self.canvas.create_image(0, 0, anchor=tk.NW, image=photo)
            self.canvas.image = photo  # Keep the reference
        else:
            self.canvas.delete("all")
```

```python
    def process_and_display_frame(self):
        if self.video and self.frame_index >= 0 and self.frame_index < len(self.video):
            try:
                frame_data = self.video.get_data(self.frame_index)
                frame = cv2.cvtColor(frame_data, cv2.COLOR_RGB2BGR)
                self.process_frame(frame)
            except IndexError:
                print(f"Frame index {self.frame_index} is out of range.")
                self.paused = True  # Pause to prevent further errors
            except Exception as e:
                print(f"Error processing frame: {e}")
                self.paused = True
        self.update_frame_label()

    def next_frame(self):
        if self.video and self.frame_index < len(self.video) - 1:  # Check if next frame exists
            self.frame_index += 1
            self.process_and_display_frame()
        else:
            print("No more frames to display.")
            self.paused = True

    def prev_frame(self):
        if self.video and self.frame_index > 0:
            self.frame_index -= 1
            self.process_and_display_frame()
        else:
            print("Already at the first frame.")
            self.paused = True

    def update_frame_label(self):
        self.frame_label.config(text=f"Frame: {self.frame_index}")

    def on_mousewheel(self, event):
        direction = event.delta // 120
        current_value = int(self.zoom_scale.get())
        if direction == 1 and current_value < 10:
            current_value += 1
        elif direction == -1 and current_value > 1:
            current_value -= 1
        self.zoom_scale.set(current_value)
        self.update_zoom()

    def on_press(self, event):
        self.tracker = None
```

```python
        self.start_x = self.canvas.canvasx(event.x)
        self.start_y = self.canvas.canvasy(event.y)
        # Clear the previous bounding box if it exists
        if self.bbox_rect:
            self.canvas.delete(self.bbox_rect)
            self.bbox_rect = None
        self.bbox = None
        self.bbox2 = None

    def on_drag(self, event):
        # Update the endpoint of the rectangle as the mouse moves
        cur_x = self.canvas.canvasx(event.x)
        cur_y = self.canvas.canvasy(event.y)

        # Define the coordinates correctly ensuring x1 < x2 and y1 < y2
        x1, y1 = min(self.start_x, cur_x), min(self.start_y, cur_y)
        x2, y2 = max(self.start_x, cur_x), max(self.start_y, cur_y)

        # Update dimensions for tracking
        self.initial_w = x2 - x1
        self.initial_h = y2 - y1
        self.bbox = (x1, y1, self.initial_w, self.initial_h)
        self.bbox2 = (self.start_x, self.start_y, cur_x, cur_y)

        # Update or create a rectangle on the canvas
        if self.bbox_rect:
            self.canvas.coords(self.bbox_rect, x1, y1, x2, y2)
        else:
            self.bbox_rect = self.canvas.create_rectangle(x1, y1, x2, y2, outline="red", width=6)

    def on_release(self, event):
        self.analyze_histogram()  # Call analyze_histogram() method when the mouse button is released

    def analyze_histogram(self):
        if self.bbox2 is not None and self.video:
            x1, y1, x2, y2 = map(int, self.bbox2)
            if x1 != x2 and y1 != y2:
                try:
                    frame = self.video.get_data(self.frame_index)
                    # Ensure the bounding box is within the frame boundaries
                    h, w, _ = frame.shape
                    x1, x2 = max(0, min(x1, w)), max(0, min(x2, w))
                    y1, y2 = max(0, min(y1, h)), max(0, min(y2, h))

                    # Ensure x1 < x2 and y1 < y2
                    x1, x2 = sorted([x1, x2])
```

```python
                    y1, y2 = sorted([y1, y2])

                    cropped_frame = frame[y1:y2, x1:x2]
                    if cropped_frame.size > 0:
                        cropped_frame = cv2.cvtColor(cropped_frame, cv2.COLOR_BGR2RGB)

                        # Get selected filter from combobox
                        selected_filter = self.filter_combobox.get()
                        # Apply selected filter
                        filtered_frame = self.apply_filter(selected_filter, cropped_frame)

                        self.create_popup_window(filtered_frame)
                        self.display_cropped_image(filtered_frame)
                        self.display_histograms(filtered_frame)
                    else:
                        print("Cropped frame is empty.")
                except Exception as e:
                    print("Failed to process frame:", e)
            else:
                print("Bounding box dimensions are zero or negative.")

    def create_popup_window(self, cropped_frame):
        self.popup_window = tk.Toplevel(self.master)
        self.popup_window.title("Cropped Image and Its Histogram")
        self.popup_window.geometry("1500x700")


    def display_cropped_image(self, cropped_frame):
        cropped_frame_frame = tk.Frame(self.popup_window)
        cropped_frame_frame.pack(side="left")

        cropped_frame_rgb = cv2.cvtColor(cropped_frame, cv2.COLOR_BGR2RGB)
        cropped_img = Image.fromarray(cropped_frame_rgb)
        cropped_img = cropped_img.resize((600, 600))

        cropped_photo = ImageTk.PhotoImage(cropped_img)
        cropped_canvas = tk.Canvas(cropped_frame_frame, width=600, height=600)
        cropped_canvas.pack(side="left", anchor="nw")
        cropped_canvas.create_image(0, 0, anchor="nw", image=cropped_photo)
        cropped_canvas.image = cropped_photo

    def display_histograms(self, cropped_frame):
        histograms_frame = tk.Frame(self.popup_window)
        histograms_frame.pack(side="right", padx=20)
```

```python
        self.display_line_histogram(cropped_frame, histograms_frame)
        self.display_bar_histogram(cropped_frame, histograms_frame)

    def display_line_histogram(self, cropped_frame, histograms_frame):
        line_histogram_frame = tk.Frame(histograms_frame)
        line_histogram_frame.pack(side="top", pady=10)

        plt.figure(figsize=(12, 4))
        color = ('r', 'g', 'b')
        for i, col in enumerate(color):
            histr = cv2.calcHist([cropped_frame], [i], None, [256], [0, 256])
            plt.plot(histr, color=col, label=f'Channel {col.upper()}', linewidth=2)
            plt.xlim([0, 256])
        plt.title('Line Histogram')
        plt.xlabel('Pixel Value')
        plt.ylabel('Frequency')
        plt.tight_layout()
        plt.grid(True)
        plt.legend()

        line_histogram_img = self.plot_to_image(plt)
        self.display_histogram_image(line_histogram_frame, line_histogram_img)

    def display_bar_histogram(self, cropped_frame, histograms_frame):
        bar_histogram_frame = tk.Frame(histograms_frame)
        bar_histogram_frame.pack(side="bottom", pady=10)

        plt.figure(figsize=(12, 4))
        color = ('r', 'g', 'b')
        for i, col in enumerate(color):
            hist_range = (0, 256)
            hist_counts, _ = np.histogram(cropped_frame[:, :, i], bins=64, range=hist_range)
            plt.bar(np.arange(64), hist_counts, color=col, alpha=0.7, label=f'Channel {col.upper()}')
            for index, value in enumerate(hist_counts):
                plt.text(index, value + 10, str(int(value)), ha='center', va='bottom', fontsize=9)

        plt.title('Bar Histogram')
        plt.xlabel('Pixel Value')
        plt.ylabel('Frequency')
        plt.xticks(np.linspace(0, 63, num=5), np.linspace(0, 255, num=5, dtype=int)) # Adjust x-axis ticks
        plt.tight_layout()
        plt.grid(True)
        plt.legend()
```

```python
        bar_histogram_img = self.plot_to_image(plt)
        self.display_histogram_image(bar_histogram_frame, bar_histogram_img)

    def display_histogram_image(self, parent_frame, img):
        histogram_photo = ImageTk.PhotoImage(image=img)
        histogram_canvas = tk.Canvas(parent_frame, width=900, height=300)
        histogram_canvas.pack(side="bottom", anchor="se")
        histogram_canvas.create_image(0, 0, anchor="nw", image=histogram_photo)
        histogram_canvas.image = histogram_photo

    def plot_histogram_bar_to_image(self, image):
        # Calculate histogram for each channel
        histograms = []
        for i in range(3):
            hist_range = (0, 256)
            hist_counts, _ = np.histogram(image[:, :, i], bins=64, range=hist_range)  # Adjust bins to 64
            histograms.append(hist_counts)

        # Extracting only 64 bins from the histogram
        num_bins = 64  # Adjusted to 64 bins

        # Generating colors for each channel
        colors = ['red', 'green', 'blue']

        plt.figure()
        for i, histogram in enumerate(histograms):
            # Normalize the histogram counts for better visualization
            hist_counts = histogram / np.sum(histogram)
            # Setting the color for each channel
            plt.bar(np.arange(num_bins), hist_counts[:num_bins], color=colors[i], alpha=0.7, label=f'Channel {["Red", "Green", "Blue"][i]}')

        plt.xlabel('Pixel Value')
        plt.ylabel('Normalized Frequency')
        plt.title('RGB Channel Histograms')
        plt.grid(True)
        plt.tight_layout()
        plt.legend()

        # Convert the histogram bar graph to an image
        histogram_bar_img = self.plot_to_image(plt)
        histogram_bar_photo = ImageTk.PhotoImage(image=histogram_bar_img)

        return histogram_bar_photo

    def plot_to_image(self, plt):
        plt.savefig('temp_plot.png')
```

```python
        img = Image.open('temp_plot.png')
        return img

    def apply_filter(self, filter_name, frame):
        if filter_name == "None":
            return frame
        elif filter_name == "Gaussian":
            return cv2.GaussianBlur(frame, (5, 5), 0)
        elif filter_name == "Mean":
            return cv2.blur(frame, (5, 5))
        elif filter_name == "Median":
            return cv2.medianBlur(frame, 5)
        elif filter_name == "Bilateral Filtering":
            return cv2.bilateralFilter(frame, 9, 75, 75)
        elif filter_name == "Non-local Means Denoising":
            return cv2.fastNlMeansDenoisingColored(frame, None, 10, 10, 7, 21)
        elif filter_name == "Anisotropic Diffusion":
            return self.anisotropic_diffusion(frame)
        elif filter_name == "Total Variation Denoising":
            return self.total_variation_denoising(frame)
        elif filter_name == "Wiener Filter":
            return self.wiener_filter(frame)
        elif filter_name == "Adaptive Thresholding":
            return self.adaptive_threshold_each_channel(frame)
        elif filter_name == "Haar Wavelet Transform":
            return self.haar_wavelet_transform(frame)
        elif filter_name == "Daubechies Wavelet Transform":
            return self.daubechies_wavelet_transform(frame)
        else:
            return frame  # Default: return original frame if filter not found

    def wiener_filter(self, frame, kernel_size=(5, 5), noise_var=0.01):
        # Check if frame is None
        if frame is None:
            print("Error: Input frame is None.")
            return None

        # Check if frame is a valid numpy array
        if not isinstance(frame, np.ndarray):
            print("Error: Input frame is not a numpy array.")
            return None

        # Check if frame is an empty array
        if frame.size == 0:
            print("Error: Input frame is empty.")
            return None

        # Check if frame is in BGR color space
```

```python
        if frame.shape[-1] != 3:
            print("Error: Input frame is not in BGR color space.")
            return None

        # Apply Wiener filter
        filtered_frame = cv2.medianBlur(frame, kernel_size[0])  # Use kernel_size[0] as the kernel size
        filtered_frame = cv2.fastNlMeansDenoising(filtered_frame, h=noise_var)
        return filtered_frame

    def adaptive_threshold_each_channel(self, frame):
        # Split the frame into individual channels
        b, g, r = cv2.split(frame)

        # Apply adaptive thresholding to each channel separately
        b_thresh = cv2.adaptiveThreshold(b, 255, cv2.ADAPTIVE_THRESH_GAUSSIAN_C, cv2.THRESH_BINARY, 11, 2)
        g_thresh = cv2.adaptiveThreshold(g, 255, cv2.ADAPTIVE_THRESH_GAUSSIAN_C, cv2.THRESH_BINARY, 11, 2)
        r_thresh = cv2.adaptiveThreshold(r, 255, cv2.ADAPTIVE_THRESH_GAUSSIAN_C, cv2.THRESH_BINARY, 11, 2)

        # Merge the thresholded channels back together
        return cv2.merge([b_thresh, g_thresh, r_thresh])

    def haar_wavelet_transform(self, frame):
        # Split the frame into its individual color channels
        b, g, r = cv2.split(frame)

        # Perform the wavelet transform on each channel separately
        b_coeffs = pywt.dwt2(b, 'haar')
        g_coeffs = pywt.dwt2(g, 'haar')
        r_coeffs = pywt.dwt2(r, 'haar')

        # Reconstruct the channels from the coefficients
        b_reconstructed = pywt.idwt2(b_coeffs, 'haar')
        g_reconstructed = pywt.idwt2(g_coeffs, 'haar')
        r_reconstructed = pywt.idwt2(r_coeffs, 'haar')

        # Clip the values to ensure they are within the valid range
        b_reconstructed = np.clip(b_reconstructed, 0, 255).astype(np.uint8)
        g_reconstructed = np.clip(g_reconstructed, 0, 255).astype(np.uint8)
        r_reconstructed = np.clip(r_reconstructed, 0, 255).astype(np.uint8)

        # Merge the channels back together
        return cv2.merge([b_reconstructed, g_reconstructed, r_reconstructed])

    def daubechies_wavelet_transform(self, frame):
```

```python
        # Split the frame into its individual color channels
        b, g, r = cv2.split(frame)

        # Choose the wavelet function (Daubechies 5)
        wavelet = 'db5'

        # Perform the wavelet transform on each channel separately
        b_coeffs = pywt.dwt2(b, wavelet)
        g_coeffs = pywt.dwt2(g, wavelet)
        r_coeffs = pywt.dwt2(r, wavelet)

        # Reconstruct the channels from the coefficients
        b_reconstructed = pywt.idwt2(b_coeffs, wavelet)
        g_reconstructed = pywt.idwt2(g_coeffs, wavelet)
        r_reconstructed = pywt.idwt2(r_coeffs, wavelet)

        # Clip the values to ensure they are within the valid range
        b_reconstructed = np.clip(b_reconstructed, 0, 255).astype(np.uint8)
        g_reconstructed = np.clip(g_reconstructed, 0, 255).astype(np.uint8)
        r_reconstructed = np.clip(r_reconstructed, 0, 255).astype(np.uint8)

        # Merge the channels back together
        return cv2.merge([b_reconstructed, g_reconstructed, r_reconstructed])

    def anisotropic_diffusion(self, img):
        return cv2.fastNlMeansDenoisingColored(img, None, 10, 10, 7, 21)

    def apply_total_variation_denoising_channel(self, channel, weight, iterations):
        # Initialize the result with the original channel
        result = channel.copy().astype(np.float64)  # Convert to float64

        # Perform total variation denoising
        for _ in range(iterations):
            # Compute the gradient of the channel
            dx = cv2.Sobel(result, cv2.CV_64F, 1, 0, ksize=3)
            dy = cv2.Sobel(result, cv2.CV_64F, 0, 1, ksize=3)

            # Update the channel using the gradient and the weight
            result -= weight * np.sqrt(dx**2 + dy**2)

        # Clip the values to ensure they are within the valid range
        result = np.clip(result, 0, 255).astype(np.uint8)

        return result

    def total_variation_denoising(self, img, weight=0.01, iterations=20):
        # Split the image into its individual color channels
        b, g, r = cv2.split(img)
```

```python
        # Apply total variation denoising to each channel separately
        b_denoised = self.apply_total_variation_denoising_channel(b, weight, iterations)
        g_denoised = self.apply_total_variation_denoising_channel(g, weight, iterations)
        r_denoised = self.apply_total_variation_denoising_channel(r, weight, iterations)

        # Merge the denoised channels back together
        return cv2.merge([b_denoised, g_denoised, r_denoised])
def main():
    root = tk.Tk()
    app = KDEWithFilter(root)
    root.mainloop()

if __name__ == "__main__":
    main()
```

MOTION DETECTION WITH K-NEAREST NEIGHBORS (KNN)

DESCRIPTION

The project is a sophisticated motion detection system that utilizes the K-Nearest Neighbors (KNN) algorithm for background subtraction, implemented through a user-friendly graphical interface using Tkinter. This system is designed to detect and highlight movement within video streams, making it a valuable tool for surveillance and monitoring activities.

At the core of the application is the KNN background subtractor, which dynamically distinguishes between the background and moving objects. This method is particularly effective because it adapts over time, improving its accuracy in various lighting conditions and minimizing false detections caused by minor changes in the environment.

The user interface is structured to provide an interactive experience. It includes a display frame where the video is played and analyzed in real-time. The frame is accompanied by a listbox displaying detected motion events, allowing users to see a log of all movements captured during the video playback. Various control buttons are integrated, such as play, pause, stop, and frame navigation, enhancing the user's ability to closely inspect any segment of the video.

An additional feature is the application's ability to apply various filters to the video frames. These filters range from simple Gaussian blurring to more complex methods like anisotropic diffusion and wavelet transforms. This functionality not only allows for experimentation with different preprocessing techniques but also helps in improving the quality of the motion detection under different scenarios.

When motion is detected, the software processes the frame to highlight the moving objects using bounding boxes. These are then labeled and listed in the sidebar, providing easy tracking of movement within the video. Each detected object is numbered, making it easier to follow and review movement patterns throughout the playback.

For advanced analysis, the application offers tools like zoom and custom area selection. Users can draw a rectangle over the video to focus on a specific area, and upon releasing the mouse button, the selected area can be subjected to further analysis such as histogram evaluation. This feature is invaluable for detailed study of motion or color distributions within a specified region.

The combination of real-time video processing with interactive controls and advanced analytical tools makes this application extremely versatile. Whether it's for security surveillance, traffic monitoring, or simply studying motion dynamics in videos, the system provides robust functionality packaged within an intuitive graphical interface.

PROCESSING FRAME

```python
def process_frame(self, frame):
    gray = cv2.cvtColor(frame, cv2.COLOR_BGR2GRAY)
    gray = cv2.GaussianBlur(gray, (21, 21), 0)  # Blur to reduce noise

    # Apply the KNN model to get the foreground mask
    fg_mask = self.knn_subtractor.apply(gray)

    # Optional: apply additional threshold to clean up the foreground mask
    _, fg_mask = cv2.threshold(fg_mask, self.threshold, 255, cv2.THRESH_BINARY)

    # Dilate the thresholded image to fill in holes, helping in better contour detection
    fg_mask = cv2.dilate(fg_mask, None, iterations=2)

    # Find contours on the thresholded image to detect moving objects
    contours, _ = cv2.findContours(fg_mask, cv2.RETR_EXTERNAL, cv2.CHAIN_APPROX_SIMPLE)

    self.listbox.delete(0, tk.END)  # Clear existing entries in the listbox
    box_number = 0  # Initialize box number

    # Loop over the contours
    for contour in contours:
        if cv2.contourArea(contour) < 500:
            continue  # Ignore small contours
        box_number += 1  # Increment the box number for each contour
        (x, y, w, h) = cv2.boundingRect(contour)
        center_x, center_y = x + w // 2, y + h // 2
        cv2.rectangle(frame, (x, y), (x+w, y+h), (50, 0, 255), 2)
        self.listbox.insert(tk.END, f"Box {box_number}: Center ({center_x}, {center_y})")
        cv2.putText(frame, f"{box_number}", (x + 5, y + 20), cv2.FONT_HERSHEY_SIMPLEX, 0.6, (0, 255, 0), 2)

    self.display_frame(frame)
```

The process_frame() method in your application is a critical part of the motion detection system using the K-Nearest Neighbors (KNN) algorithm. Here's a breakdown of how this function works:

1. Convert to Grayscale: The video frame is converted to grayscale using cv2.cvtColor(frame, cv2.COLOR_BGR2GRAY). Grayscale conversion is essential as it simplifies the processing by reducing the amount of data (three color channels down to one), which is particularly useful for motion detection.
2. Noise Reduction: A Gaussian blur is applied to the grayscale image (cv2.GaussianBlur(gray, (21, 21), 0)). This step helps to reduce noise and detail in the image, which can improve the accuracy of the motion detection by smoothing out the variations and highlighting significant movements.
3. Foreground Mask Application: The KNN background subtractor is applied to the blurred grayscale image to create a foreground mask (fg_mask = self.knn_subtractor.apply(gray)). This mask differentiates between the static background and the moving objects by identifying areas of the frame that have changed.
4. Thresholding: The foreground mask is then thresholded (_, fg_mask = cv2.threshold(fg_mask, self.threshold, 255, cv2.THRESH_BINARY)). This step converts the grayscale mask into a binary image, where the white pixels represent moving objects and the black pixels represent the background.
5. Image Dilation: The binary image undergoes dilation (cv2.dilate(fg_mask, None, iterations=2)). Dilation enlarges the white areas and closes small holes within detected objects, which helps in forming better contours in the next step.
6. Contour Detection: Contours are detected in the dilated image using cv2.findContours(fg_mask, cv2.RETR_EXTERNAL, cv2.CHAIN_APPROX_SIMPLE). Contours are used to outline the moving objects, allowing the system to compute their boundaries accurately.
7. Loop Over Contours: For each contour detected, the area is checked to ensure it is significant enough to be considered (if cv2.contourArea(contour) < 500: continue). Small contours are ignored to avoid noise. For each valid contour, a bounding rectangle is calculated and drawn around the detected object. The center of each box

is calculated and displayed, along with a numeric identifier for each detected movement.

8. Update Display: The modified frame, now with rectangles and labels around detected moving objects, is displayed on the canvas using the self.display_frame(frame) method. This visual feedback is crucial for users monitoring the video stream.

Overall, this method effectively highlights moving objects within a video stream in real-time, providing a robust tool for surveillance and activity monitoring within various environments.

RUNNING PROGRAM

Run program and click on Play/Pause button. Or, you can choose certain frame by pushing Next Frame button. Then, draw a bounding box rectangle on certain object in the frame and push Next Frame button.

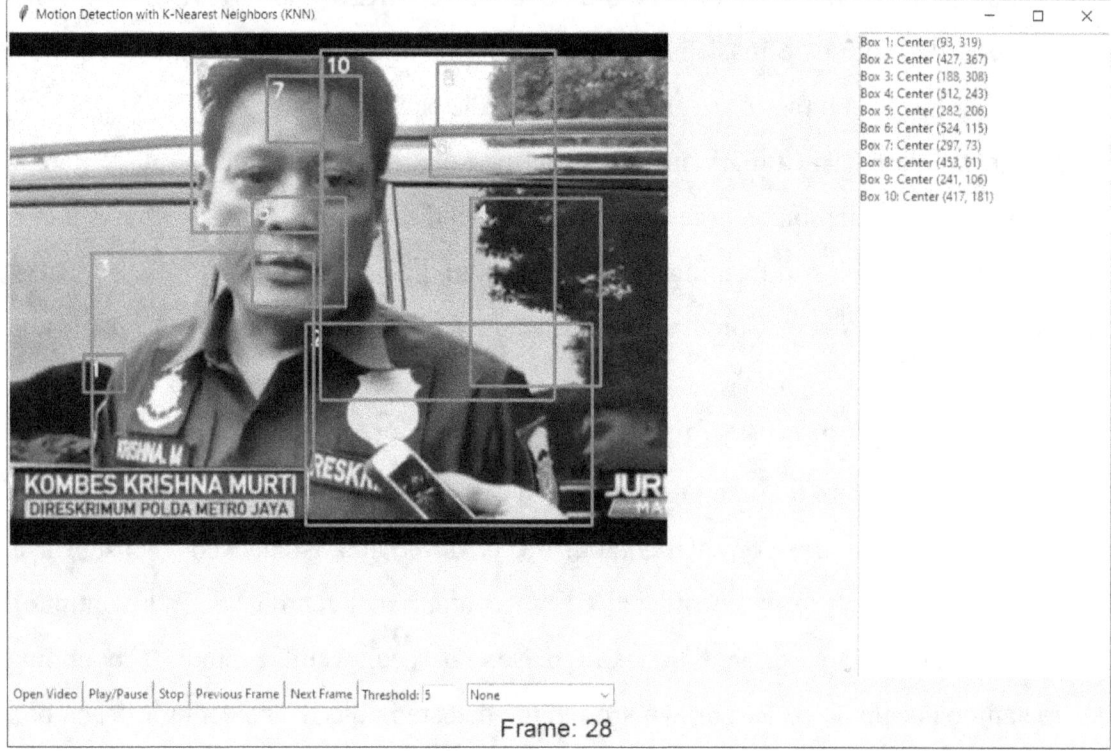

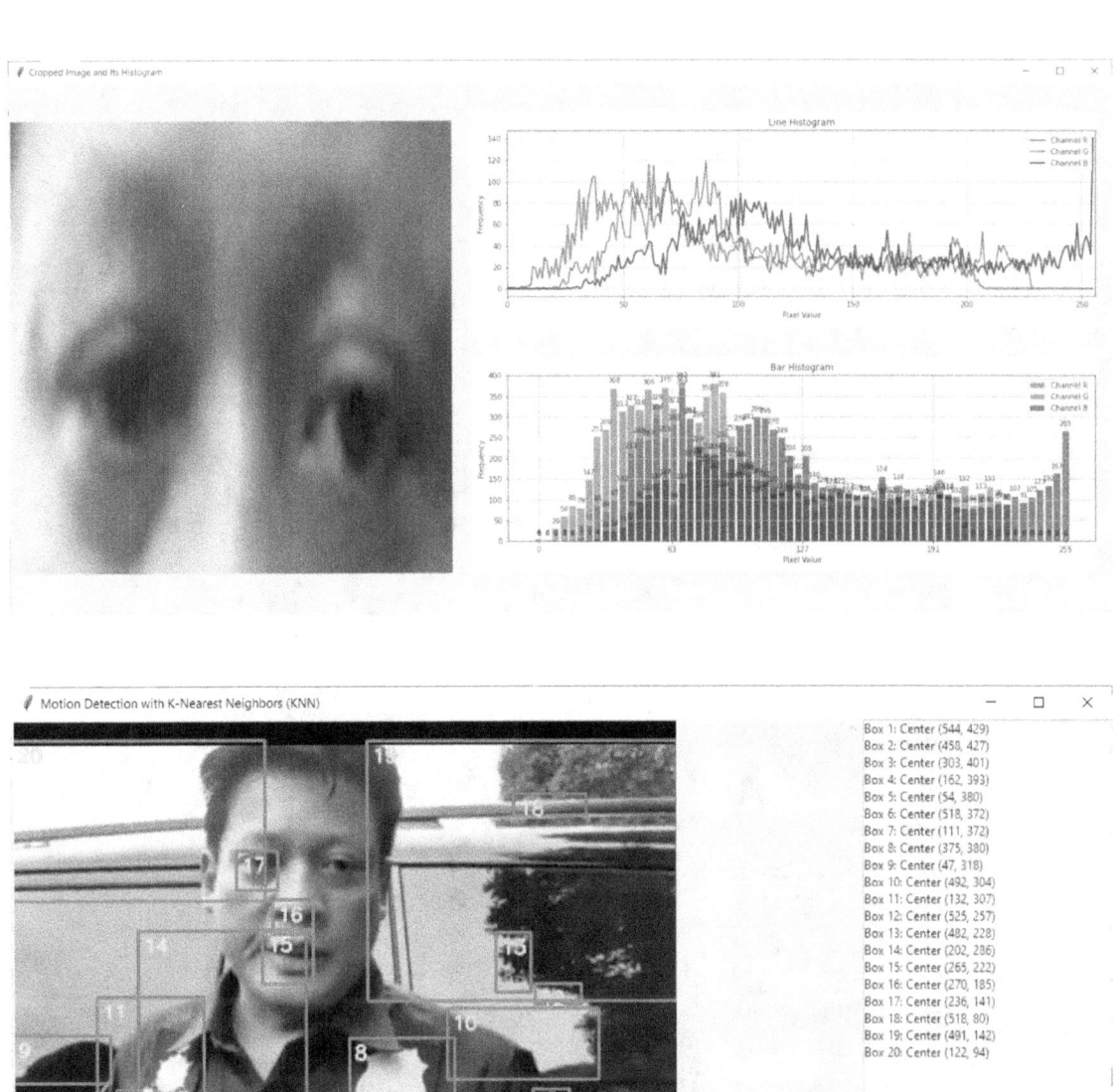

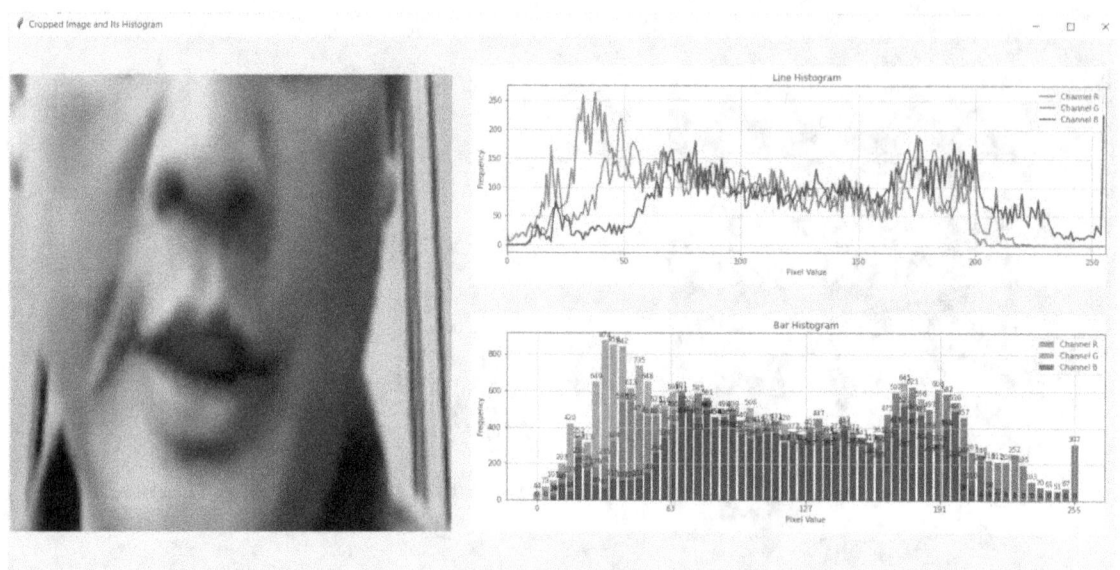

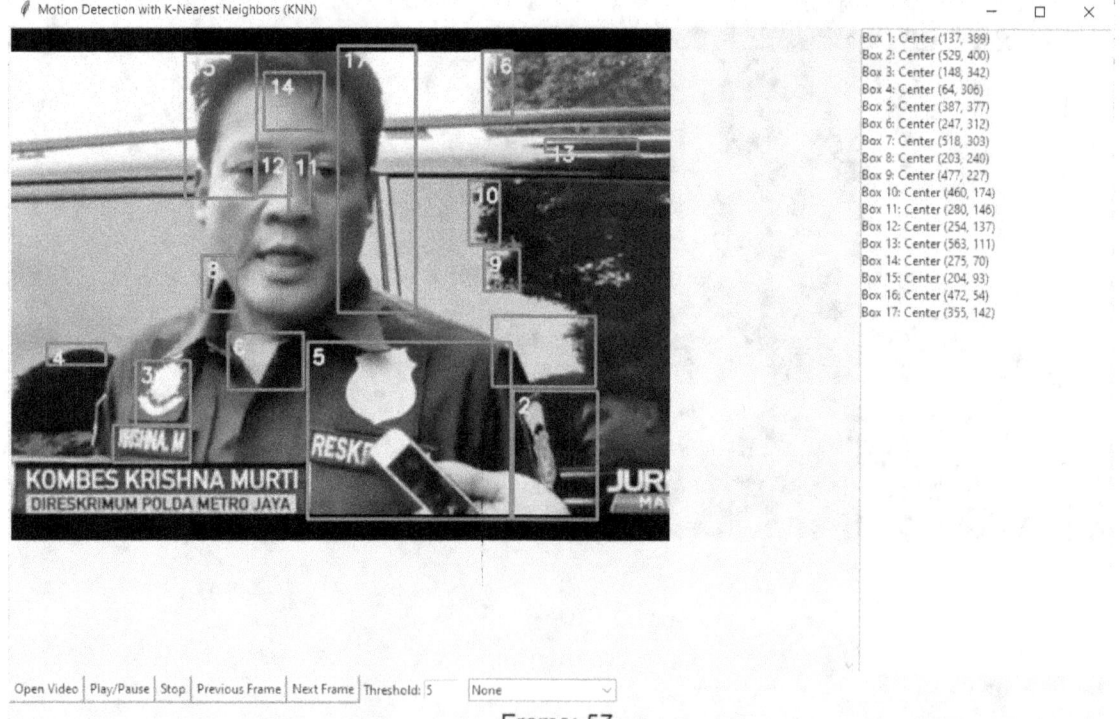

SOURCE CODE

```python
#knn_with_filtering.py
import tkinter as tk
from tkinter import ttk
from tkinter import filedialog
from PIL import Image, ImageTk
import cv2
import imageio
import matplotlib.pyplot as plt
import pywt
import numpy as np

class MixtureofGaussiansWithFilter:
    def __init__(self, master):
        self.master = master
        self.master.title("Motion Detection with K-Nearest Neighbors (KNN)")
        self.bbox_rect = None  # Initialize bbox_rect attribute to None

        # Initialize the KNN background subtractor
        self.knn_subtractor = cv2.createBackgroundSubtractorKNN(detectShadows=True)

        # Video related variables
        self.video = None
        self.previous_frame = None
        self.frame_index = 0
        self.paused = True
        self.threshold = 5  # Default threshold for frame differencing

        # Creates widgets
        self.create_widgets(master)

    def create_widgets(self, master):
        # Create a frame for the canvas and listbox
        display_frame = tk.Frame(master)
        display_frame.pack(fill=tk.BOTH, expand=True)

        # Set up the canvas
        self.canvas = tk.Canvas(display_frame, width=800, height=600)
        self.canvas.pack(side=tk.LEFT, fill=tk.BOTH, expand=True)
        self.canvas.bind("<MouseWheel>", self.on_mousewheel)
        self.canvas.bind("<ButtonPress-1>", self.on_press)
        self.canvas.bind("<B1-Motion>", self.on_drag)
        self.canvas.bind("<ButtonRelease-1>", self.on_release)  # Bind ButtonRelease event
```

```python
        # Set up the listbox for displaying centers
        self.listbox = tk.Listbox(display_frame, width=40, height=20)
        self.listbox.pack(side=tk.RIGHT, fill=tk.Y)

        # Add scrollbar to the listbox
        scrollbar = tk.Scrollbar(display_frame, orient="vertical", command=self.listbox.yview)
        scrollbar.pack(side=tk.RIGHT, fill=tk.Y)
        self.listbox.config(yscrollcommand=scrollbar.set)

        # Control Panel below the display frame
        control_panel = tk.Frame(master)
        control_panel.pack(fill=tk.X)

        self.open_button = tk.Button(control_panel, text="Open Video", command=self.open_video)
        self.open_button.pack(side=tk.LEFT)

        self.play_button = tk.Button(control_panel, text="Play/Pause", command=self.toggle_play_pause)
        self.play_button.pack(side=tk.LEFT)

        self.stop_button = tk.Button(control_panel, text="Stop", command=self.stop_video)
        self.stop_button.pack(side=tk.LEFT)

        self.prev_button = tk.Button(control_panel, text="Previous Frame", command=self.prev_frame)
        self.prev_button.pack(side=tk.LEFT)

        self.next_button = tk.Button(control_panel, text="Next Frame", command=self.next_frame)
        self.next_button.pack(side=tk.LEFT)

        # Frame number label
        self.frame_label = tk.Label(master, text="Frame: 0", font=('Helvetica', 18))
        self.frame_label.pack()

        # Threshold Control
        self.threshold_label = tk.Label(control_panel, text="Threshold:")
        self.threshold_label.pack(side=tk.LEFT)

        self.threshold_entry = tk.Entry(control_panel, width=5)
        self.threshold_entry.pack(side=tk.LEFT)
        self.threshold_entry.insert(0, '5')  # Default threshold value
        self.threshold_entry.bind("<Return>", self.update_threshold)

        # Available filters
```

```python
        self.filters = ["None", "Gaussian", "Mean", "Median", "Bilateral Filtering",
                        "Non-local Means Denoising", "Anisotropic Diffusion",
                        "Total Variation Denoising", "Wiener Filter",
                        "Adaptive Thresholding", "Haar Wavelet Transform",
                        "Daubechies Wavelet Transform"]

        # Subframe for complex controls such as combobox
        filter_frame = tk.Frame(control_panel)
        filter_frame.pack(side=tk.LEFT, fill=tk.X, expand=True)

        # Combobox for Selecting Filters
        self.filter_combobox = ttk.Combobox(filter_frame, values=self.filters)
        self.filter_combobox.pack(side=tk.LEFT, padx=10, pady=5)
        self.filter_combobox.current(0)  # Set default value

    def update_threshold(self, event):
        try:
            self.threshold = int(self.threshold_entry.get())
            print(f"Threshold updated to {self.threshold}")
        except ValueError:
            print("Invalid input for threshold. Please enter an integer.")

    def open_video(self):
        video_path = filedialog.askopenfilename(filetypes=[("Video files",
"*.mp4;*.avi;*.mkv;*.wmv")])
        if video_path:
            self.video = imageio.get_reader(video_path)
            self.frame_index = 0
            self.previous_frame = None
            self.paused = False
            self.play_video()
            self.update_frame_label()

    def toggle_play_pause(self):
        self.paused = not self.paused
        if not self.paused:
            self.play_video()

    def stop_video(self):
        self.paused = True
        self.frame_index = 0
        self.previous_frame = None
        self.update_frame_label()
        self.display_frame(None)  # Clear the canvas

    def play_video(self):
        if not self.paused and self.video:
            if self.frame_index < len(self.video):
```

```python
            try:
                frame_data = self.video.get_data(self.frame_index)
                frame = cv2.cvtColor(frame_data, cv2.COLOR_RGB2BGR)
                self.process_frame(frame)
                self.frame_index += 1
                self.master.after(42, self.play_video)  # Schedule next frame
            except IndexError:
                print("Reached the end of the video.")
                self.paused = True  # Stop the video playback
            self.update_frame_label()

    def process_frame(self, frame):
        gray = cv2.cvtColor(frame, cv2.COLOR_BGR2GRAY)
        gray = cv2.GaussianBlur(gray, (21, 21), 0)  # Blur to reduce noise

        # Apply the KNN model to get the foreground mask
        fg_mask = self.knn_subtractor.apply(gray)

        # Optional: apply additional threshold to clean up the foreground mask
        _, fg_mask = cv2.threshold(fg_mask, self.threshold, 255, cv2.THRESH_BINARY)

        # Dilate the thresholded image to fill in holes, helping in better contour detection
        fg_mask = cv2.dilate(fg_mask, None, iterations=2)

        # Find contours on the thresholded image to detect moving objects
        contours, _ = cv2.findContours(fg_mask, cv2.RETR_EXTERNAL, cv2.CHAIN_APPROX_SIMPLE)

        self.listbox.delete(0, tk.END)  # Clear existing entries in the listbox
        box_number = 0  # Initialize box number

        # Loop over the contours
        for contour in contours:
            if cv2.contourArea(contour) < 500:
                continue  # Ignore small contours
            box_number += 1  # Increment the box number for each contour
            (x, y, w, h) = cv2.boundingRect(contour)
            center_x, center_y = x + w // 2, y + h // 2
            cv2.rectangle(frame, (x, y), (x+w, y+h), (50, 0, 255), 2)
            self.listbox.insert(tk.END, f"Box {box_number}: Center ({center_x}, {center_y})")
            cv2.putText(frame, f"{box_number}", (x + 5, y + 20), cv2.FONT_HERSHEY_SIMPLEX, 0.6, (0, 255, 0), 2)

        self.display_frame(frame)

    def display_frame(self, frame):
```

```python
        if frame is not None:
            image = cv2.cvtColor(frame, cv2.COLOR_BGR2RGB)
            image = Image.fromarray(image)
            photo = ImageTk.PhotoImage(image=image)
            self.canvas.create_image(0, 0, anchor=tk.NW, image=photo)
            self.canvas.image = photo  # Keep the reference
        else:
            self.canvas.delete("all")

    def process_and_display_frame(self):
        if self.video and self.frame_index >= 0 and self.frame_index < len(self.video):
            try:
                frame_data = self.video.get_data(self.frame_index)
                frame = cv2.cvtColor(frame_data, cv2.COLOR_RGB2BGR)
                self.process_frame(frame)
            except IndexError:
                print(f"Frame index {self.frame_index} is out of range.")
                self.paused = True  # Pause to prevent further errors
            except Exception as e:
                print(f"Error processing frame: {e}")
                self.paused = True
            self.update_frame_label()

    def next_frame(self):
        if self.video and self.frame_index < len(self.video) - 1:  # Check if next frame exists
            self.frame_index += 1
            self.process_and_display_frame()
        else:
            print("No more frames to display.")
            self.paused = True

    def prev_frame(self):
        if self.video and self.frame_index > 0:
            self.frame_index -= 1
            self.process_and_display_frame()
        else:
            print("Already at the first frame.")
            self.paused = True


    def update_frame_label(self):
        self.frame_label.config(text=f"Frame: {self.frame_index}")

    def on_mousewheel(self, event):
        direction = event.delta // 120
        current_value = int(self.zoom_scale.get())
```

```python
            if direction == 1 and current_value < 10:
                current_value += 1
            elif direction == -1 and current_value > 1:
                current_value -= 1
            self.zoom_scale.set(current_value)
            self.update_zoom()

    def on_press(self, event):
        self.tracker = None
        self.start_x = self.canvas.canvasx(event.x)
        self.start_y = self.canvas.canvasy(event.y)
        # Clear the previous bounding box if it exists
        if self.bbox_rect:
            self.canvas.delete(self.bbox_rect)
            self.bbox_rect = None
        self.bbox = None
        self.bbox2 = None

    def on_drag(self, event):
        # Update the endpoint of the rectangle as the mouse moves
        cur_x = self.canvas.canvasx(event.x)
        cur_y = self.canvas.canvasy(event.y)

        # Define the coordinates correctly ensuring x1 < x2 and y1 < y2
        x1, y1 = min(self.start_x, cur_x), min(self.start_y, cur_y)
        x2, y2 = max(self.start_x, cur_x), max(self.start_y, cur_y)

        # Update dimensions for tracking
        self.initial_w = x2 - x1
        self.initial_h = y2 - y1
        self.bbox = (x1, y1, self.initial_w, self.initial_h)
        self.bbox2 = (self.start_x, self.start_y, cur_x, cur_y)

        # Update or create a rectangle on the canvas
        if self.bbox_rect:
            self.canvas.coords(self.bbox_rect, x1, y1, x2, y2)
        else:
            self.bbox_rect = self.canvas.create_rectangle(x1, y1, x2, y2, outline="cyan", width=6)

    def on_release(self, event):
        self.analyze_histogram()  # Call analyze_histogram() method when the mouse button is released

    def analyze_histogram(self):
        if self.bbox2 is not None and self.video:
            x1, y1, x2, y2 = map(int, self.bbox2)
            if x1 != x2 and y1 != y2:
```

```python
            try:
                frame = self.video.get_data(self.frame_index)
                # Ensure the bounding box is within the frame boundaries
                h, w, _ = frame.shape
                x1, x2 = max(0, min(x1, w)), max(0, min(x2, w))
                y1, y2 = max(0, min(y1, h)), max(0, min(y2, h))

                # Ensure x1 < x2 and y1 < y2
                x1, x2 = sorted([x1, x2])
                y1, y2 = sorted([y1, y2])

                cropped_frame = frame[y1:y2, x1:x2]
                if cropped_frame.size > 0:
                    cropped_frame = cv2.cvtColor(cropped_frame, cv2.COLOR_BGR2RGB)

                    # Get selected filter from combobox
                    selected_filter = self.filter_combobox.get()
                    # Apply selected filter
                    filtered_frame = self.apply_filter(selected_filter, cropped_frame)

                    self.create_popup_window(filtered_frame)
                    self.display_cropped_image(filtered_frame)
                    self.display_histograms(filtered_frame)
                else:
                    print("Cropped frame is empty.")
            except Exception as e:
                print("Failed to process frame:", e)
        else:
            print("Bounding box dimensions are zero or negative.")


def create_popup_window(self, cropped_frame):
    self.popup_window = tk.Toplevel(self.master)
    self.popup_window.title("Cropped Image and Its Histogram")
    self.popup_window.geometry("1500x700")


def display_cropped_image(self, cropped_frame):
    cropped_frame_frame = tk.Frame(self.popup_window)
    cropped_frame_frame.pack(side="left")

    cropped_frame_rgb = cv2.cvtColor(cropped_frame, cv2.COLOR_BGR2RGB)
    cropped_img = Image.fromarray(cropped_frame_rgb)
    cropped_img = cropped_img.resize((600, 600))

    cropped_photo = ImageTk.PhotoImage(cropped_img)
```

```python
        cropped_canvas = tk.Canvas(cropped_frame_frame, width=600, height=600)
        cropped_canvas.pack(side="left", anchor="nw")
        cropped_canvas.create_image(0, 0, anchor="nw", image=cropped_photo)
        cropped_canvas.image = cropped_photo

    def display_histograms(self, cropped_frame):
        histograms_frame = tk.Frame(self.popup_window)
        histograms_frame.pack(side="right", padx=20)

        self.display_line_histogram(cropped_frame, histograms_frame)
        self.display_bar_histogram(cropped_frame, histograms_frame)

    def display_line_histogram(self, cropped_frame, histograms_frame):
        line_histogram_frame = tk.Frame(histograms_frame)
        line_histogram_frame.pack(side="top", pady=10)

        plt.figure(figsize=(12, 4))
        color = ('r', 'g', 'b')
        for i, col in enumerate(color):
            histr = cv2.calcHist([cropped_frame], [i], None, [256], [0, 256])
            plt.plot(histr, color=col, label=f'Channel {col.upper()}', linewidth=2)
            plt.xlim([0, 256])
        plt.title('Line Histogram')
        plt.xlabel('Pixel Value')
        plt.ylabel('Frequency')
        plt.tight_layout()
        plt.grid(True)
        plt.legend()

        line_histogram_img = self.plot_to_image(plt)
        self.display_histogram_image(line_histogram_frame, line_histogram_img)

    def display_bar_histogram(self, cropped_frame, histograms_frame):
        bar_histogram_frame = tk.Frame(histograms_frame)
        bar_histogram_frame.pack(side="bottom", pady=10)

        plt.figure(figsize=(12, 4))
        color = ('r', 'g', 'b')
        for i, col in enumerate(color):
            hist_range = (0, 256)
            hist_counts, _ = np.histogram(cropped_frame[:, :, i], bins=64, range=hist_range)
            plt.bar(np.arange(64), hist_counts, color=col, alpha=0.7, label=f'Channel {col.upper()}')
            for index, value in enumerate(hist_counts):
                plt.text(index, value + 10, str(int(value)), ha='center', va='bottom', fontsize=9)
```

```python
        plt.title('Bar Histogram')
        plt.xlabel('Pixel Value')
        plt.ylabel('Frequency')
        plt.xticks(np.linspace(0, 63, num=5), np.linspace(0, 255, num=5, dtype=int)) # Adjust x-axis ticks
        plt.tight_layout()
        plt.grid(True)
        plt.legend()

        bar_histogram_img = self.plot_to_image(plt)
        self.display_histogram_image(bar_histogram_frame, bar_histogram_img)

    def display_histogram_image(self, parent_frame, img):
        histogram_photo = ImageTk.PhotoImage(image=img)
        histogram_canvas = tk.Canvas(parent_frame, width=900, height=300)
        histogram_canvas.pack(side="bottom", anchor="se")
        histogram_canvas.create_image(0, 0, anchor="nw", image=histogram_photo)
        histogram_canvas.image = histogram_photo

    def plot_histogram_bar_to_image(self, image):
        # Calculate histogram for each channel
        histograms = []
        for i in range(3):
            hist_range = (0, 256)
            hist_counts, _ = np.histogram(image[:, :, i], bins=64, range=hist_range) # Adjust bins to 64
            histograms.append(hist_counts)

        # Extracting only 64 bins from the histogram
        num_bins = 64  # Adjusted to 64 bins

        # Generating colors for each channel
        colors = ['red', 'green', 'blue']

        plt.figure()
        for i, histogram in enumerate(histograms):
            # Normalize the histogram counts for better visualization
            hist_counts = histogram / np.sum(histogram)
            # Setting the color for each channel
            plt.bar(np.arange(num_bins), hist_counts[:num_bins], color=colors[i], alpha=0.7, label=f'Channel {["Red", "Green", "Blue"][i]}')

        plt.xlabel('Pixel Value')
        plt.ylabel('Normalized Frequency')
        plt.title('RGB Channel Histograms')
        plt.grid(True)
        plt.tight_layout()
        plt.legend()
```

```python
        # Convert the histogram bar graph to an image
        histogram_bar_img = self.plot_to_image(plt)
        histogram_bar_photo = ImageTk.PhotoImage(image=histogram_bar_img)

        return histogram_bar_photo

    def plot_to_image(self, plt):
        plt.savefig('temp_plot.png')
        img = Image.open('temp_plot.png')
        return img

    def apply_filter(self, filter_name, frame):
        if filter_name == "None":
            return frame
        elif filter_name == "Gaussian":
            return cv2.GaussianBlur(frame, (5, 5), 0)
        elif filter_name == "Mean":
            return cv2.blur(frame, (5, 5))
        elif filter_name == "Median":
            return cv2.medianBlur(frame, 5)
        elif filter_name == "Bilateral Filtering":
            return cv2.bilateralFilter(frame, 9, 75, 75)
        elif filter_name == "Non-local Means Denoising":
            return cv2.fastNlMeansDenoisingColored(frame, None, 10, 10, 7, 21)
        elif filter_name == "Anisotropic Diffusion":
            return self.anisotropic_diffusion(frame)
        elif filter_name == "Total Variation Denoising":
            return self.total_variation_denoising(frame)
        elif filter_name == "Wiener Filter":
            return self.wiener_filter(frame)
        elif filter_name == "Adaptive Thresholding":
            return self.adaptive_threshold_each_channel(frame)
        elif filter_name == "Haar Wavelet Transform":
            return self.haar_wavelet_transform(frame)
        elif filter_name == "Daubechies Wavelet Transform":
            return self.daubechies_wavelet_transform(frame)
        else:
            return frame  # Default: return original frame if filter not found

    def wiener_filter(self, frame, kernel_size=(5, 5), noise_var=0.01):
        # Check if frame is None
        if frame is None:
            print("Error: Input frame is None.")
            return None

        # Check if frame is a valid numpy array
        if not isinstance(frame, np.ndarray):
```

```python
            print("Error: Input frame is not a numpy array.")
            return None

        # Check if frame is an empty array
        if frame.size == 0:
            print("Error: Input frame is empty.")
            return None

        # Check if frame is in BGR color space
        if frame.shape[-1] != 3:
            print("Error: Input frame is not in BGR color space.")
            return None

        # Apply Wiener filter
        filtered_frame = cv2.medianBlur(frame, kernel_size[0])  # Use kernel_size[0] as the kernel size
        filtered_frame = cv2.fastNlMeansDenoising(filtered_frame, h=noise_var)
        return filtered_frame

    def adaptive_threshold_each_channel(self, frame):
        # Split the frame into individual channels
        b, g, r = cv2.split(frame)

        # Apply adaptive thresholding to each channel separately
        b_thresh = cv2.adaptiveThreshold(b, 255, cv2.ADAPTIVE_THRESH_GAUSSIAN_C, cv2.THRESH_BINARY, 11, 2)
        g_thresh = cv2.adaptiveThreshold(g, 255, cv2.ADAPTIVE_THRESH_GAUSSIAN_C, cv2.THRESH_BINARY, 11, 2)
        r_thresh = cv2.adaptiveThreshold(r, 255, cv2.ADAPTIVE_THRESH_GAUSSIAN_C, cv2.THRESH_BINARY, 11, 2)

        # Merge the thresholded channels back together
        return cv2.merge([b_thresh, g_thresh, r_thresh])

    def haar_wavelet_transform(self, frame):
        # Split the frame into its individual color channels
        b, g, r = cv2.split(frame)

        # Perform the wavelet transform on each channel separately
        b_coeffs = pywt.dwt2(b, 'haar')
        g_coeffs = pywt.dwt2(g, 'haar')
        r_coeffs = pywt.dwt2(r, 'haar')

        # Reconstruct the channels from the coefficients
        b_reconstructed = pywt.idwt2(b_coeffs, 'haar')
        g_reconstructed = pywt.idwt2(g_coeffs, 'haar')
        r_reconstructed = pywt.idwt2(r_coeffs, 'haar')
```

```python
        # Clip the values to ensure they are within the valid range
        b_reconstructed = np.clip(b_reconstructed, 0, 255).astype(np.uint8)
        g_reconstructed = np.clip(g_reconstructed, 0, 255).astype(np.uint8)
        r_reconstructed = np.clip(r_reconstructed, 0, 255).astype(np.uint8)

        # Merge the channels back together
        return cv2.merge([b_reconstructed, g_reconstructed, r_reconstructed])

    def daubechies_wavelet_transform(self, frame):
        # Split the frame into its individual color channels
        b, g, r = cv2.split(frame)

        # Choose the wavelet function (Daubechies 5)
        wavelet = 'db5'

        # Perform the wavelet transform on each channel separately
        b_coeffs = pywt.dwt2(b, wavelet)
        g_coeffs = pywt.dwt2(g, wavelet)
        r_coeffs = pywt.dwt2(r, wavelet)

        # Reconstruct the channels from the coefficients
        b_reconstructed = pywt.idwt2(b_coeffs, wavelet)
        g_reconstructed = pywt.idwt2(g_coeffs, wavelet)
        r_reconstructed = pywt.idwt2(r_coeffs, wavelet)

        # Clip the values to ensure they are within the valid range
        b_reconstructed = np.clip(b_reconstructed, 0, 255).astype(np.uint8)
        g_reconstructed = np.clip(g_reconstructed, 0, 255).astype(np.uint8)
        r_reconstructed = np.clip(r_reconstructed, 0, 255).astype(np.uint8)

        # Merge the channels back together
        return cv2.merge([b_reconstructed, g_reconstructed, r_reconstructed])

    def anisotropic_diffusion(self, img):
        return cv2.fastNlMeansDenoisingColored(img, None, 10, 10, 7, 21)

    def apply_total_variation_denoising_channel(self, channel, weight, iterations):
        # Initialize the result with the original channel
        result = channel.copy().astype(np.float64)  # Convert to float64

        # Perform total variation denoising
        for _ in range(iterations):
            # Compute the gradient of the channel
            dx = cv2.Sobel(result, cv2.CV_64F, 1, 0, ksize=3)
            dy = cv2.Sobel(result, cv2.CV_64F, 0, 1, ksize=3)

            # Update the channel using the gradient and the weight
            result -= weight * np.sqrt(dx**2 + dy**2)
```

```python
        # Clip the values to ensure they are within the valid range
        result = np.clip(result, 0, 255).astype(np.uint8)

        return result

    def total_variation_denoising(self, img, weight=0.01, iterations=20):
        # Split the image into its individual color channels
        b, g, r = cv2.split(img)

        # Apply total variation denoising to each channel separately
        b_denoised = self.apply_total_variation_denoising_channel(b, weight, iterations)
        g_denoised = self.apply_total_variation_denoising_channel(g, weight, iterations)
        r_denoised = self.apply_total_variation_denoising_channel(r, weight, iterations)

        # Merge the denoised channels back together
        return cv2.merge([b_denoised, g_denoised, r_denoised])
def main():
    root = tk.Tk()
    app = MixtureofGaussiansWithFilter(root)
    root.mainloop()

if __name__ == "__main__":
    main()
```

MOTION DETECTION WITH MEDIAN FILTERING

DESCRIPTION

The "Median Filtering with Filtering" project involves a sophisticated motion detection application developed using Python and a range of libraries including Tkinter for the graphical user interface, OpenCV for image processing, and ImageIO for video handling. The application is designed to help users monitor video feeds and detect motion in real-time, making it suitable for security purposes, wildlife observation, or any scenario where movement tracking is necessary.

At the heart of this application lies the use of median filtering, a method effective at reducing noise from video frames. This process smooths out the image, making it easier to identify changes between frames, which are indicative of motion. The median filter works by replacing each pixel value in the frame with the median value of the pixels in a small neighborhood around it. This method is particularly good at preserving edges while removing noise, making it ideal for preparing frames for motion detection.

The application's user interface is robust, featuring controls to load and play video streams, and tools to pause, stop, restart, and navigate through the video. Users can adjust the sensitivity of motion detection by changing the threshold settings, which affects how motion is detected and displayed. There's also a list box that logs coordinates of detected movements, enhancing user interaction by allowing them to see a log of all movements detected during a session.

Advanced filtering options are integrated into the application, allowing users to apply different types of image filters such as Gaussian, bilateral, and non-local means denoising. This feature provides flexibility in handling different types of video qualities and noise levels, making the tool versatile across various environments and lighting conditions. Each filter can be selected via a dropdown menu, providing an easy way for users to experiment with different settings to see which works best for their specific needs.

Additionally, the project is structured to support further expansion and customization. Developers can add more filters, enhance the GUI, or integrate more complex motion detection algorithms as needed. The use of Python and its libraries ensures that the application remains accessible and modifiable, catering to both novice programmers and experienced developers looking to tailor the application to specific use cases or integrate it into larger systems.

PROCESSING FRAME

```python
def process_frame(self, frame):
    # Convert the frame to grayscale
    gray = cv2.cvtColor(frame, cv2.COLOR_BGR2GRAY)

    # Apply median filtering to reduce noise
    gray = cv2.medianBlur(gray, 5)  # The kernel size can be adjusted depending on the noise level

    if self.running_average is None:
        self.running_average = gray.astype("float")
        return  # Skip the rest until the running average is initialized

    # Update the running average
    cv2.accumulateWeighted(gray, self.running_average, 0.05)

    # Compute the difference between the current frame and the running average
    frame_delta = cv2.absdiff(gray, cv2.convertScaleAbs(self.running_average))

    # Threshold the delta image
    thresh = cv2.threshold(frame_delta, self.threshold, 255, cv2.THRESH_BINARY)[1]
    thresh = cv2.dilate(thresh, None, iterations=2)  # Dilate the thresholded image to fill in holes

    # Find contours on the thresholded image
    contours, _ = cv2.findContours(thresh.copy(), cv2.RETR_EXTERNAL, cv2.CHAIN_APPROX_SIMPLE)

    self.listbox.delete(0, tk.END)  # Clear existing entries in the listbox
    box_number = 0  # Initialize box number

    # Loop over the contours
    for contour in contours:
        if cv2.contourArea(contour) < 500:
            continue  # Ignore small contours
        box_number += 1  # Increment the box number for each contour
        (x, y, w, h) = cv2.boundingRect(contour)
        center_x, center_y = x + w // 2, y + h // 2
        cv2.rectangle(frame, (x, y), (x+w, y+h), (50, 0, 255), 2)
        self.listbox.insert(tk.END, f"Box {box_number}: Center ({center_x}, {center_y})")
        cv2.putText(frame, f"{box_number}", (x + 5, y + 20), cv2.FONT_HERSHEY_SIMPLEX, 0.6, (0, 255, 0), 2)
```

```
self.display_frame(frame)
```

The method process_frame() is a crucial part of a video processing application, specifically designed for motion detection within a series of video frames. Here's a step-by-step breakdown of what each part of the method does:

1. Convert to Grayscale: The first step involves converting the incoming video frame from color (BGR) to grayscale. Grayscale simplifies the image data by reducing it to shades of gray, thereby reducing computational requirements for the subsequent operations.

2. Apply Median Filtering: This step helps reduce noise in the grayscale image. Median filtering is particularly effective at removing "salt and pepper" noise without blurring the edges of objects within the frame. The kernel size of 5 is typically sufficient for mild noise, but it can be adjusted based on specific needs and the noise level of the input video.

3. Initialize or Update Running Average: If the running average of frames (self.running_average) hasn't been initialized, it's set up using the current frame's data. If it already exists, the method updates this running average using a weighted accumulation. Here, the weight of 0.05 indicates how much influence the current frame has on the average. This running average helps in differentiating between background and moving objects across frames.

4. Compute Frame Difference: The difference between the current grayscale frame and the running average is calculated. This difference highlights areas of the frame where significant changes have occurred—typically areas with motion.

5. Threshold and Dilate Image: The frame difference is then thresholded to create a binary image where the white areas represent motion. The cv2.dilate operation is applied afterward, which helps fill in gaps in the detected motion areas, making the detection more cohesive and less fragmented.

6. Detect Contours: This step involves finding all contiguous regions (contours) in the thresholded image, which correspond to areas of motion. The method scans through

these contours to identify significant movements by ignoring small, irrelevant changes which are smaller than a predefined area (500 pixels in this case).

7. Annotate and Record Movements: For every significant contour, a bounding box is drawn around the area of motion, and details such as the box number and the center coordinates of the motion are added to the listbox for user reference. This allows users to see a log of detected motions, making the application interactive and useful for surveillance or monitoring activities.

8. Display the Frame: Finally, the processed frame, now annotated with rectangles and text identifying detected motions, is displayed on the GUI. This visual feedback is crucial for users to verify and observe motion detection performance in real-time.

Overall, this method embodies a comprehensive approach to motion detection using basic image processing techniques, suitable for applications in security systems, wildlife monitoring, or any scenario requiring automated motion tracking.

RUNNING PROGRAM

Run program and click on Play/Pause button. Or, you can choose certain frame by pushing Next Frame button. Then, draw a bounding box rectangle on certain object in the frame and push Next Frame button.

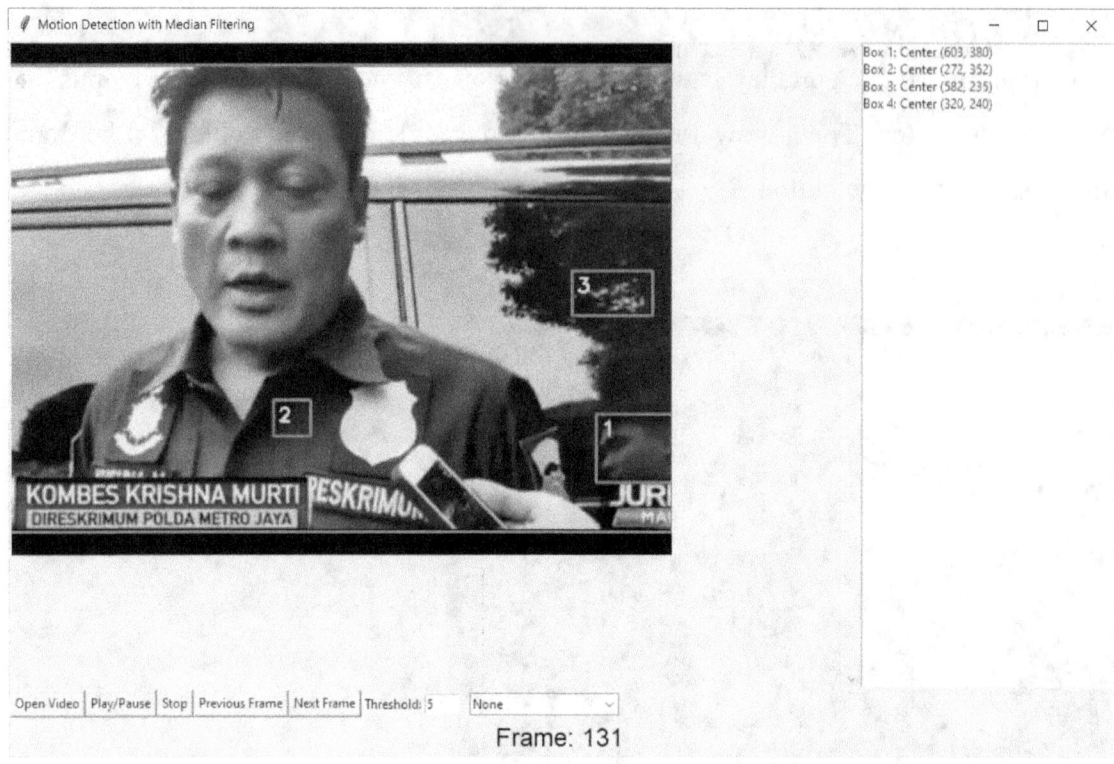

SOURCE CODE

```
#median_filtering_with_filtering.py
import tkinter as tk
from tkinter import ttk
from tkinter import filedialog
from PIL import Image, ImageTk
import cv2
import imageio
import matplotlib.pyplot as plt
import pywt
import numpy as np

class MedianFilteringWithFilter:
    def __init__(self, master):
        self.master = master
        self.master.title("Motion Detection with Median Filtering")
        self.bbox_rect = None  # Initialize bbox_rect attribute to None
```

```python
        self.running_average = None  # Stores the running average of frames

        # Video related variables
        self.video = None
        self.previous_frame = None
        self.frame_index = 0
        self.paused = True
        self.threshold = 5  # Default threshold for frame differencing

        # Creates widgets
        self.create_widgets(master)

    def create_widgets(self, master):
        # Create a frame for the canvas and listbox
        display_frame = tk.Frame(master)
        display_frame.pack(fill=tk.BOTH, expand=True)

        # Set up the canvas
        self.canvas = tk.Canvas(display_frame, width=800, height=600)
        self.canvas.pack(side=tk.LEFT, fill=tk.BOTH, expand=True)
        self.canvas.bind("<MouseWheel>", self.on_mousewheel)
        self.canvas.bind("<ButtonPress-1>", self.on_press)
        self.canvas.bind("<B1-Motion>", self.on_drag)
        self.canvas.bind("<ButtonRelease-1>", self.on_release)  # Bind ButtonRelease event

        # Set up the listbox for displaying centers
        self.listbox = tk.Listbox(display_frame, width=40, height=20)
        self.listbox.pack(side=tk.RIGHT, fill=tk.Y)

        # Add scrollbar to the listbox
        scrollbar = tk.Scrollbar(display_frame, orient="vertical", command=self.listbox.yview)
        scrollbar.pack(side=tk.RIGHT, fill=tk.Y)
        self.listbox.config(yscrollcommand=scrollbar.set)

        # Control Panel below the display frame
        control_panel = tk.Frame(master)
        control_panel.pack(fill=tk.X)

        self.open_button = tk.Button(control_panel, text="Open Video", command=self.open_video)
        self.open_button.pack(side=tk.LEFT)

        self.play_button = tk.Button(control_panel, text="Play/Pause", command=self.toggle_play_pause)
        self.play_button.pack(side=tk.LEFT)
```

```python
        self.stop_button = tk.Button(control_panel, text="Stop", 
command=self.stop_video)
        self.stop_button.pack(side=tk.LEFT)

        self.prev_button = tk.Button(control_panel, text="Previous Frame", 
command=self.prev_frame)
        self.prev_button.pack(side=tk.LEFT)

        self.next_button = tk.Button(control_panel, text="Next Frame", 
command=self.next_frame)
        self.next_button.pack(side=tk.LEFT)

        # Frame number label
        self.frame_label = tk.Label(master, text="Frame: 0", font=('Helvetica', 18))
        self.frame_label.pack()

        # Threshold Control
        self.threshold_label = tk.Label(control_panel, text="Threshold:")
        self.threshold_label.pack(side=tk.LEFT)

        self.threshold_entry = tk.Entry(control_panel, width=5)
        self.threshold_entry.pack(side=tk.LEFT)
        self.threshold_entry.insert(0, '5')  # Default threshold value
        self.threshold_entry.bind("<Return>", self.update_threshold)

        # Available filters
        self.filters = ["None", "Gaussian", "Mean", "Median", "Bilateral Filtering",
                        "Non-local Means Denoising", "Anisotropic Diffusion",
                        "Total Variation Denoising", "Wiener Filter",
                        "Adaptive Thresholding", "Haar Wavelet Transform",
                        "Daubechies Wavelet Transform"]

        # Subframe for complex controls such as combobox
        filter_frame = tk.Frame(control_panel)
        filter_frame.pack(side=tk.LEFT, fill=tk.X, expand=True)

        # Combobox for Selecting Filters
        self.filter_combobox = ttk.Combobox(filter_frame, values=self.filters)
        self.filter_combobox.pack(side=tk.LEFT, padx=10, pady=5)
        self.filter_combobox.current(0)  # Set default value

    def update_threshold(self, event):
        try:
            self.threshold = int(self.threshold_entry.get())
            print(f"Threshold updated to {self.threshold}")
        except ValueError:
            print("Invalid input for threshold. Please enter an integer.")
```

```python
    def open_video(self):
        video_path = filedialog.askopenfilename(filetypes=[("Video files",
"*.mp4;*.avi;*.mkv;*.wmv")])
        if video_path:
            self.video = imageio.get_reader(video_path)
            self.frame_index = 0
            self.previous_frame = None
            self.paused = False
            self.play_video()
            self.update_frame_label()

    def toggle_play_pause(self):
        self.paused = not self.paused
        if not self.paused:
            self.play_video()

    def stop_video(self):
        self.paused = True
        self.frame_index = 0
        self.previous_frame = None
        self.update_frame_label()
        self.display_frame(None)  # Clear the canvas

    def play_video(self):
        if not self.paused and self.video:
            if self.frame_index < len(self.video):
                try:
                    frame_data = self.video.get_data(self.frame_index)
                    frame = cv2.cvtColor(frame_data, cv2.COLOR_RGB2BGR)
                    self.process_frame(frame)
                    self.frame_index += 1
                    self.master.after(42, self.play_video)  # Schedule next frame
                except IndexError:
                    print("Reached the end of the video.")
                    self.paused = True  # Stop the video playback
                self.update_frame_label()

    def process_frame(self, frame):
        # Convert the frame to grayscale
        gray = cv2.cvtColor(frame, cv2.COLOR_BGR2GRAY)

        # Apply median filtering to reduce noise
        gray = cv2.medianBlur(gray, 5)  # The kernel size can be adjusted depending
on the noise level

        if self.running_average is None:
            self.running_average = gray.astype("float")
            return  # Skip the rest until the running average is initialized
```

```python
        # Update the running average
        cv2.accumulateWeighted(gray, self.running_average, 0.05)

        # Compute the difference between the current frame and the running average
        frame_delta = cv2.absdiff(gray, cv2.convertScaleAbs(self.running_average))

        # Threshold the delta image
        thresh = cv2.threshold(frame_delta, self.threshold, 255, cv2.THRESH_BINARY)[1]
        thresh = cv2.dilate(thresh, None, iterations=2)  # Dilate the thresholded image to fill in holes

        # Find contours on the thresholded image
        contours, _ = cv2.findContours(thresh.copy(), cv2.RETR_EXTERNAL, cv2.CHAIN_APPROX_SIMPLE)

        self.listbox.delete(0, tk.END)  # Clear existing entries in the listbox
        box_number = 0  # Initialize box number

        # Loop over the contours
        for contour in contours:
            if cv2.contourArea(contour) < 500:
                continue  # Ignore small contours
            box_number += 1  # Increment the box number for each contour
            (x, y, w, h) = cv2.boundingRect(contour)
            center_x, center_y = x + w // 2, y + h // 2
            cv2.rectangle(frame, (x, y), (x+w, y+h), (50, 0, 255), 2)
            self.listbox.insert(tk.END, f"Box {box_number}: Center ({center_x}, {center_y})")
            cv2.putText(frame, f"{box_number}", (x + 5, y + 20), cv2.FONT_HERSHEY_SIMPLEX, 0.6, (0, 255, 0), 2)

        self.display_frame(frame)

    def display_frame(self, frame):
        if frame is not None:
            image = cv2.cvtColor(frame, cv2.COLOR_BGR2RGB)
            image = Image.fromarray(image)
            photo = ImageTk.PhotoImage(image=image)
            self.canvas.create_image(0, 0, anchor=tk.NW, image=photo)
            self.canvas.image = photo  # Keep the reference
        else:
            self.canvas.delete("all")

    def process_and_display_frame(self):
        if self.video and self.frame_index >= 0 and self.frame_index < len(self.video):
```

```python
            try:
                frame_data = self.video.get_data(self.frame_index)
                frame = cv2.cvtColor(frame_data, cv2.COLOR_RGB2BGR)
                self.process_frame(frame)
            except IndexError:
                print(f"Frame index {self.frame_index} is out of range.")
                self.paused = True  # Pause to prevent further errors
            except Exception as e:
                print(f"Error processing frame: {e}")
                self.paused = True
            self.update_frame_label()

    def next_frame(self):
        if self.video and self.frame_index < len(self.video) - 1:  # Check if next frame exists
            self.frame_index += 1
            self.process_and_display_frame()
        else:
            print("No more frames to display.")
            self.paused = True

    def prev_frame(self):
        if self.video and self.frame_index > 0:
            self.frame_index -= 1
            self.process_and_display_frame()
        else:
            print("Already at the first frame.")
            self.paused = True


    def update_frame_label(self):
        self.frame_label.config(text=f"Frame: {self.frame_index}")

    def on_mousewheel(self, event):
        direction = event.delta // 120
        current_value = int(self.zoom_scale.get())
        if direction == 1 and current_value < 10:
            current_value += 1
        elif direction == -1 and current_value > 1:
            current_value -= 1
        self.zoom_scale.set(current_value)
        self.update_zoom()

    def on_press(self, self, event):
        self.tracker = None
        self.start_x = self.canvas.canvasx(event.x)
        self.start_y = self.canvas.canvasy(event.y)
        # Clear the previous bounding box if it exists
```

```python
            if self.bbox_rect:
                self.canvas.delete(self.bbox_rect)
                self.bbox_rect = None
        self.bbox = None
        self.bbox2 = None

    def on_drag(self, event):
        # Update the endpoint of the rectangle as the mouse moves
        cur_x = self.canvas.canvasx(event.x)
        cur_y = self.canvas.canvasy(event.y)

        # Define the coordinates correctly ensuring x1 < x2 and y1 < y2
        x1, y1 = min(self.start_x, cur_x), min(self.start_y, cur_y)
        x2, y2 = max(self.start_x, cur_x), max(self.start_y, cur_y)

        # Update dimensions for tracking
        self.initial_w = x2 - x1
        self.initial_h = y2 - y1
        self.bbox = (x1, y1, self.initial_w, self.initial_h)
        self.bbox2 = (self.start_x, self.start_y, cur_x, cur_y)

        # Update or create a rectangle on the canvas
        if self.bbox_rect:
            self.canvas.coords(self.bbox_rect, x1, y1, x2, y2)
        else:
            self.bbox_rect = self.canvas.create_rectangle(x1, y1, x2, y2,
outline="cyan", width=6)

    def on_release(self, event):
        self.analyze_histogram()  # Call analyze_histogram() method when the mouse
button is released

    def analyze_histogram(self):
        if self.bbox2 is not None and self.video:
            x1, y1, x2, y2 = map(int, self.bbox2)
            if x1 != x2 and y1 != y2:
                try:
                    frame = self.video.get_data(self.frame_index)
                    # Ensure the bounding box is within the frame boundaries
                    h, w, _ = frame.shape
                    x1, x2 = max(0, min(x1, w)), max(0, min(x2, w))
                    y1, y2 = max(0, min(y1, h)), max(0, min(y2, h))

                    # Ensure x1 < x2 and y1 < y2
                    x1, x2 = sorted([x1, x2])
                    y1, y2 = sorted([y1, y2])

                    cropped_frame = frame[y1:y2, x1:x2]
```

```python
                    if cropped_frame.size > 0:
                        cropped_frame = cv2.cvtColor(cropped_frame, 
cv2.COLOR_BGR2RGB)

                        # Get selected filter from combobox
                        selected_filter = self.filter_combobox.get()
                        # Apply selected filter
                        filtered_frame = self.apply_filter(selected_filter, 
cropped_frame)

                        self.create_popup_window(filtered_frame)
                        self.display_cropped_image(filtered_frame)
                        self.display_histograms(filtered_frame)
                    else:
                        print("Cropped frame is empty.")
                except Exception as e:
                    print("Failed to process frame:", e)
            else:
                print("Bounding box dimensions are zero or negative.")


    def create_popup_window(self, cropped_frame):
        self.popup_window = tk.Toplevel(self.master)
        self.popup_window.title("Cropped Image and Its Histogram")
        self.popup_window.geometry("1500x700")



    def display_cropped_image(self, cropped_frame):
        cropped_frame_frame = tk.Frame(self.popup_window)
        cropped_frame_frame.pack(side="left")

        cropped_frame_rgb = cv2.cvtColor(cropped_frame, cv2.COLOR_BGR2RGB)
        cropped_img = Image.fromarray(cropped_frame_rgb)
        cropped_img = cropped_img.resize((600, 600))

        cropped_photo = ImageTk.PhotoImage(cropped_img)
        cropped_canvas = tk.Canvas(cropped_frame_frame, width=600, height=600)
        cropped_canvas.pack(side="left", anchor="nw")
        cropped_canvas.create_image(0, 0, anchor="nw", image=cropped_photo)
        cropped_canvas.image = cropped_photo

    def display_histograms(self, cropped_frame):
        histograms_frame = tk.Frame(self.popup_window)
        histograms_frame.pack(side="right", padx=20)

        self.display_line_histogram(cropped_frame, histograms_frame)
        self.display_bar_histogram(cropped_frame, histograms_frame)
```

```python
    def display_line_histogram(self, cropped_frame, histograms_frame):
        line_histogram_frame = tk.Frame(histograms_frame)
        line_histogram_frame.pack(side="top", pady=10)

        plt.figure(figsize=(12, 4))
        color = ('r', 'g', 'b')
        for i, col in enumerate(color):
            histr = cv2.calcHist([cropped_frame], [i], None, [256], [0, 256])
            plt.plot(histr, color=col, label=f'Channel {col.upper()}', linewidth=2)
            plt.xlim([0, 256])
        plt.title('Line Histogram')
        plt.xlabel('Pixel Value')
        plt.ylabel('Frequency')
        plt.tight_layout()
        plt.grid(True)
        plt.legend()

        line_histogram_img = self.plot_to_image(plt)
        self.display_histogram_image(line_histogram_frame, line_histogram_img)

    def display_bar_histogram(self, cropped_frame, histograms_frame):
        bar_histogram_frame = tk.Frame(histograms_frame)
        bar_histogram_frame.pack(side="bottom", pady=10)

        plt.figure(figsize=(12, 4))
        color = ('r', 'g', 'b')
        for i, col in enumerate(color):
            hist_range = (0, 256)
            hist_counts, _ = np.histogram(cropped_frame[:, :, i], bins=64, range=hist_range)
            plt.bar(np.arange(64), hist_counts, color=col, alpha=0.7, label=f'Channel {col.upper()}')
            for index, value in enumerate(hist_counts):
                plt.text(index, value + 10, str(int(value)), ha='center', va='bottom', fontsize=9)

        plt.title('Bar Histogram')
        plt.xlabel('Pixel Value')
        plt.ylabel('Frequency')
        plt.xticks(np.linspace(0, 63, num=5), np.linspace(0, 255, num=5, dtype=int))  # Adjust x-axis ticks
        plt.tight_layout()
        plt.grid(True)
        plt.legend()

        bar_histogram_img = self.plot_to_image(plt)
        self.display_histogram_image(bar_histogram_frame, bar_histogram_img)
```

```python
    def display_histogram_image(self, parent_frame, img):
        histogram_photo = ImageTk.PhotoImage(image=img)
        histogram_canvas = tk.Canvas(parent_frame, width=900, height=300)
        histogram_canvas.pack(side="bottom", anchor="se")
        histogram_canvas.create_image(0, 0, anchor="nw", image=histogram_photo)
        histogram_canvas.image = histogram_photo

    def plot_histogram_bar_to_image(self, image):
        # Calculate histogram for each channel
        histograms = []
        for i in range(3):
            hist_range = (0, 256)
            hist_counts, _ = np.histogram(image[:, :, i], bins=64, range=hist_range)  # Adjust bins to 64
            histograms.append(hist_counts)

        # Extracting only 64 bins from the histogram
        num_bins = 64  # Adjusted to 64 bins

        # Generating colors for each channel
        colors = ['red', 'green', 'blue']

        plt.figure()
        for i, histogram in enumerate(histograms):
            # Normalize the histogram counts for better visualization
            hist_counts = histogram / np.sum(histogram)
            # Setting the color for each channel
            plt.bar(np.arange(num_bins), hist_counts[:num_bins], color=colors[i], alpha=0.7, label=f'Channel {["Red", "Green", "Blue"][i]}')

        plt.xlabel('Pixel Value')
        plt.ylabel('Normalized Frequency')
        plt.title('RGB Channel Histograms')
        plt.grid(True)
        plt.tight_layout()
        plt.legend()

        # Convert the histogram bar graph to an image
        histogram_bar_img = self.plot_to_image(plt)
        histogram_bar_photo = ImageTk.PhotoImage(image=histogram_bar_img)

        return histogram_bar_photo

    def plot_to_image(self, plt):
        plt.savefig('temp_plot.png')
        img = Image.open('temp_plot.png')
        return img
```

```python
def apply_filter(self, filter_name, frame):
    if filter_name == "None":
        return frame
    elif filter_name == "Gaussian":
        return cv2.GaussianBlur(frame, (5, 5), 0)
    elif filter_name == "Mean":
        return cv2.blur(frame, (5, 5))
    elif filter_name == "Median":
        return cv2.medianBlur(frame, 5)
    elif filter_name == "Bilateral Filtering":
        return cv2.bilateralFilter(frame, 9, 75, 75)
    elif filter_name == "Non-local Means Denoising":
        return cv2.fastNlMeansDenoisingColored(frame, None, 10, 10, 7, 21)
    elif filter_name == "Anisotropic Diffusion":
        return self.anisotropic_diffusion(frame)
    elif filter_name == "Total Variation Denoising":
        return self.total_variation_denoising(frame)
    elif filter_name == "Wiener Filter":
        return self.wiener_filter(frame)
    elif filter_name == "Adaptive Thresholding":
        return self.adaptive_threshold_each_channel(frame)
    elif filter_name == "Haar Wavelet Transform":
        return self.haar_wavelet_transform(frame)
    elif filter_name == "Daubechies Wavelet Transform":
        return self.daubechies_wavelet_transform(frame)
    else:
        return frame  # Default: return original frame if filter not found

def wiener_filter(self, frame, kernel_size=(5, 5), noise_var=0.01):
    # Check if frame is None
    if frame is None:
        print("Error: Input frame is None.")
        return None

    # Check if frame is a valid numpy array
    if not isinstance(frame, np.ndarray):
        print("Error: Input frame is not a numpy array.")
        return None

    # Check if frame is an empty array
    if frame.size == 0:
        print("Error: Input frame is empty.")
        return None

    # Check if frame is in BGR color space
    if frame.shape[-1] != 3:
        print("Error: Input frame is not in BGR color space.")
        return None
```

```python
        # Apply Wiener filter
        filtered_frame = cv2.medianBlur(frame, kernel_size[0])  # Use kernel_size[0] as the kernel size
        filtered_frame = cv2.fastNlMeansDenoising(filtered_frame, h=noise_var)
        return filtered_frame

    def adaptive_threshold_each_channel(self, frame):
        # Split the frame into individual channels
        b, g, r = cv2.split(frame)

        # Apply adaptive thresholding to each channel separately
        b_thresh = cv2.adaptiveThreshold(b, 255, cv2.ADAPTIVE_THRESH_GAUSSIAN_C, cv2.THRESH_BINARY, 11, 2)
        g_thresh = cv2.adaptiveThreshold(g, 255, cv2.ADAPTIVE_THRESH_GAUSSIAN_C, cv2.THRESH_BINARY, 11, 2)
        r_thresh = cv2.adaptiveThreshold(r, 255, cv2.ADAPTIVE_THRESH_GAUSSIAN_C, cv2.THRESH_BINARY, 11, 2)

        # Merge the thresholded channels back together
        return cv2.merge([b_thresh, g_thresh, r_thresh])

    def haar_wavelet_transform(self, frame):
        # Split the frame into its individual color channels
        b, g, r = cv2.split(frame)

        # Perform the wavelet transform on each channel separately
        b_coeffs = pywt.dwt2(b, 'haar')
        g_coeffs = pywt.dwt2(g, 'haar')
        r_coeffs = pywt.dwt2(r, 'haar')

        # Reconstruct the channels from the coefficients
        b_reconstructed = pywt.idwt2(b_coeffs, 'haar')
        g_reconstructed = pywt.idwt2(g_coeffs, 'haar')
        r_reconstructed = pywt.idwt2(r_coeffs, 'haar')

        # Clip the values to ensure they are within the valid range
        b_reconstructed = np.clip(b_reconstructed, 0, 255).astype(np.uint8)
        g_reconstructed = np.clip(g_reconstructed, 0, 255).astype(np.uint8)
        r_reconstructed = np.clip(r_reconstructed, 0, 255).astype(np.uint8)

        # Merge the channels back together
        return cv2.merge([b_reconstructed, g_reconstructed, r_reconstructed])

    def daubechies_wavelet_transform(self, frame):
        # Split the frame into its individual color channels
        b, g, r = cv2.split(frame)
```

```python
        # Choose the wavelet function (Daubechies 5)
        wavelet = 'db5'

        # Perform the wavelet transform on each channel separately
        b_coeffs = pywt.dwt2(b, wavelet)
        g_coeffs = pywt.dwt2(g, wavelet)
        r_coeffs = pywt.dwt2(r, wavelet)

        # Reconstruct the channels from the coefficients
        b_reconstructed = pywt.idwt2(b_coeffs, wavelet)
        g_reconstructed = pywt.idwt2(g_coeffs, wavelet)
        r_reconstructed = pywt.idwt2(r_coeffs, wavelet)

        # Clip the values to ensure they are within the valid range
        b_reconstructed = np.clip(b_reconstructed, 0, 255).astype(np.uint8)
        g_reconstructed = np.clip(g_reconstructed, 0, 255).astype(np.uint8)
        r_reconstructed = np.clip(r_reconstructed, 0, 255).astype(np.uint8)

        # Merge the channels back together
        return cv2.merge([b_reconstructed, g_reconstructed, r_reconstructed])

    def anisotropic_diffusion(self, img):
        return cv2.fastNlMeansDenoisingColored(img, None, 10, 10, 7, 21)

    def apply_total_variation_denoising_channel(self, channel, weight, iterations):
        # Initialize the result with the original channel
        result = channel.copy().astype(np.float64)  # Convert to float64

        # Perform total variation denoising
        for _ in range(iterations):
            # Compute the gradient of the channel
            dx = cv2.Sobel(result, cv2.CV_64F, 1, 0, ksize=3)
            dy = cv2.Sobel(result, cv2.CV_64F, 0, 1, ksize=3)

            # Update the channel using the gradient and the weight
            result -= weight * np.sqrt(dx**2 + dy**2)

        # Clip the values to ensure they are within the valid range
        result = np.clip(result, 0, 255).astype(np.uint8)

        return result

    def total_variation_denoising(self, img, weight=0.01, iterations=20):
        # Split the image into its individual color channels
        b, g, r = cv2.split(img)

        # Apply total variation denoising to each channel separately
```

```
            b_denoised = self.apply_total_variation_denoising_channel(b, weight, 
iterations)
            g_denoised = self.apply_total_variation_denoising_channel(g, weight, 
iterations)
            r_denoised = self.apply_total_variation_denoising_channel(r, weight, 
iterations)
        
            # Merge the denoised channels back together
            return cv2.merge([b_denoised, g_denoised, r_denoised])
def main():
    root = tk.Tk()
    app = MedianFilteringWithFilter(root)
    root.mainloop()

if __name__ == "__main__":
    main()
```

Bibliography

Vivian Siahaan and Rismon Hasiholan Sianipar. *TKINTER, DATA SCIENCE, AND MACHINE LEARNING*. North Sumatera: Balige Publishing, 2023.

Vivian Siahaan and Rismon Hasiholan Sianipar. *DATA VISUALIZATION, TIME-SERIES FORECASTING, AND PREDICTION USING MACHINE LEARNING WITH TKINTER*. North Sumatera: Balige Publishing, 2023.

Vivian Siahaan and Rismon Hasiholan Sianipar. *TIME-SERIES WEATHER FORECASTING AND PREDICTION USING MACHINE LEARNING WITH TKINTER*. North Sumatera: Balige Publishing, 2023.

Vivian Siahaan and Rismon Hasiholan Sianipar. DATA VISUALIZATION, TIME-SERIES FORECASTING, AND PREDICTION USING MACHINE LEARNING WITH TKINTER. North Sumatera: Balige Publishing, 2023.

Vivian Siahaan and Rismon Hasiholan Sianipar. START FROM SCRATCH DIGITAL SIGNAL PROCESSING WITH TKINTER. North Sumatera: Balige Publishing, 2023.

Vivian Siahaan and Rismon Hasiholan Sianipar. START FROM SCRATCH DIGITAL IMAGE PROCESSING WITH TKINTER. North Sumatera: Balige Publishing, 2023.

Vivian Siahaan and Rismon Hasiholan Sianipar. START FROM SCRATCH DIGITAL IMAGE PROCESSING WITH TKINTER. North Sumatera: Balige Publishing, 2023.

Vivian Siahaan and Rismon Hasiholan Sianipar. IMAGE DENOISING, EDGE DETECTION, AND SEGMENTATION WITH TKINTER. North Sumatera: Balige Publishing, 2023.

Vivian Siahaan and Rismon Hasiholan Sianipar. DIGITAL VIDEO PROCESSING PROJECTS USING PYTHON AND TKINTER. North Sumatera: Balige Publishing, 2024.

Vivian Siahaan and Rismon Hasiholan Sianipar. FRAME ANALYSIS AND PROCESSING IN DIGITAL VIDEO USING PYTHON AND TKINTER. North Sumatera: Balige Publishing, 2024.

Vivian Siahaan and Rismon Hasiholan Sianipar. MOTION ANALYSIS AND OBJECT TRACKING USING PYTHON AND TKINTER. North Sumatera: Balige Publishing, 2024.

Vivian Siahaan and Rismon Hasiholan Sianipar. FRAME FILTERING AND EDGES-DETECTION USING PYTHON AND TKINTER. North Sumatera: Balige Publishing, 2024.

Vivian Siahaan and Rismon Hasiholan Sianipar. OPTICAL FLOW ANALYSIS AND MOTION ESTIMATION IN DIGITAL VIDEO WITH PYTHON AND TKINTER. North Sumatera: Balige Publishing, 2024.

Vivian Siahaan and Rismon Hasiholan Sianipar. GRADIENT-BASED BLOCK MATCHING MOTION ESTIMATION AND OBJECT TRACKING WITH PYTHON AND TKINTER. North Sumatera: Balige Publishing, 2024.

Vivian Siahaan and Rismon Hasiholan Sianipar. FEATURES-BASED MOTION ESTIMATION AND OBJECT TRACKING WITH PYTHON AND TKINTER. North Sumatera: Balige Publishing, 2024.

www.ingramcontent.com/pod-product-compliance
Lightning Source LLC
Chambersburg PA
CBHW082204220526
45470CB00010B/3038